The LEGO® Adventure Book

Spaceships, Pirates, Dragons & More!

Megan H. Rothrock

no starch
press

San Francisco

The LEGO Adventure Book, Volume 2: Spaceships, Pirates, Dragons & More!

Copyright © 2014 by Megan H. Rothrock

First printing

Printed in China

17 16 15 14 13   1 2 3 4 5 6 7 8 9

ISBN-10: 1-59327-512-9
ISBN-13: 978-1-59327-512-9

Publisher: William Pollock
Production Editor: Serena Yang
Interior Design: Megan H. Rothrock
Featured Cover Model: Birgitte Jonsgard-Sungberg
Title Page Illustration: Gryphon
Additional Photography: Are J. Heiseldal (Chapters 3, 4, and 6) and Ian Greig (Chapter 10)
Interior Design: Megan H. Rothrock
Proofreaders: Paula L. Fleming, Laurel Chun, and Alison Law

For information on distribution, translations, or bulk sales,
please contact No Starch Press, Inc. directly:
No Starch Press, Inc.
245 8th Street, San Francisco, CA 94103
phone: 415.863.9900; fax: 415.863.9950;
info@nostarch.com; http://www.nostarch.com/

Library of Congress Cataloging-in-Publication Data
The Library of Congress Control Number for this volume is 2012033902.

Production Date: August 5, 2013
Plant & Location: Printed by Everbest Printing (Guangzhou, China), Co. Ltd
Job/Batch #: 114805

CONTENTS

AH! IT'S BEEN SO NICE TO HAVE SOME TIME BACK IN THE IDEA LAB AFTER THAT EPIC LEGO ADVENTURE! WITH SO MUCH INSPIRATION, MY PLACE SURE HAS COME A LONG WAY!

Back to the Idea Lab

Megan H. Rothrock

Nickname: megs/megzter

Profession: Author and Toy Designer

Nationality: American

Website: *www.flickr.com/photos/megzter/*

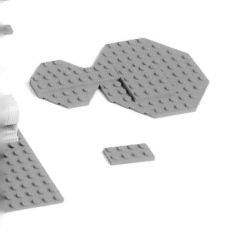

AH, THERE HE IS!

HI, NABII, GLAD YOU MADE IT!

GOOD TO SEE YOU, MEGS. IT LOOKS LIKE YOU'VE BEEN BUILDING A LOT SINCE I LAST SAW YOU.

INDEED! I HAVE BEEN KEEPING MYSELF BUSY BUILDING SINCE MY LEGO ADVENTURE! HERE, CHECK OUT SOME OF MY LATEST WORK.

I CALL THESE TWO GARDEN STATUES DRAAK AND BANDIT.

HMMM, I'VE NEVER THOUGHT OF BUILDING STATUES OF MY PETS!

HEH, I'LL SHOW YOU HOW I BUILT THEM AND SOME OTHER NEW ADDITIONS TOO!

Draak: The Iguana Statue

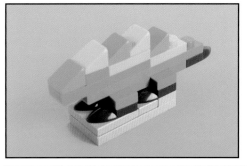
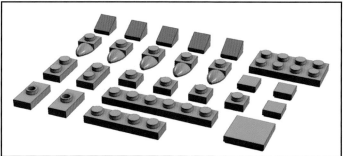

Building Tip
These LEGO models can be built in many different colors. It is fun to experiment with different color combinations.

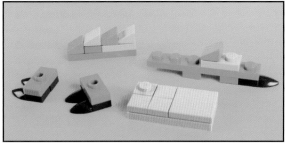
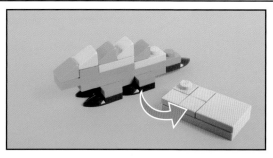
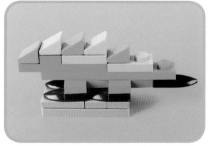

Bandit: The Bull Terrier Statue

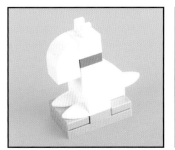
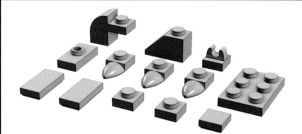
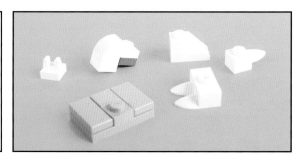

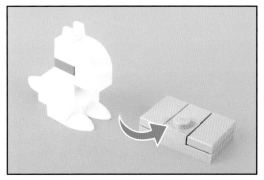

Tulips

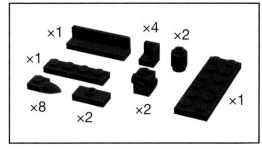
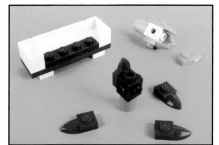

9

Greenhouse

Wheelbarrow

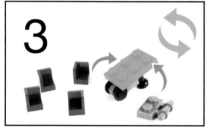 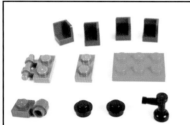  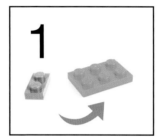

Building Tip
It's possible to be creative with LEGO bricks even if you don't have many parts. Some very interesting models can be designed using only a few carefully chosen parts.

Mailbox

   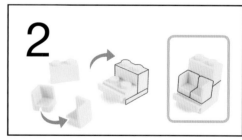

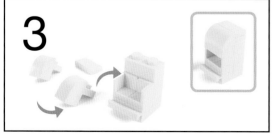  

Windmill

Thinking Tower

  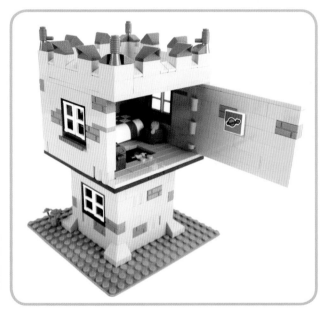

THAT'S SOME GREAT WORK THERE, MEGS.

THANKS, NABII. MY THINKING TOWER WAS INSPIRED BY DANIEL'S FROM MY FIRST LEGO ADVENTURE.

WOW! IS THAT A DRAGON ON WHEELS OVER THERE?

HEH! KIND OF. IT'S MY TRAGON! YOU KNOW, A TRAIN-DRAGON.

REALLY? THAT'S A THING?

IT IS NOW THAT I'VE IMAGINED IT! THAT'S THE BEAUTY OF LEGO BRICKS.

The Fire Tragon

LET ME SHOW YOU HOW TO BUILD MY TRAGON. YOU'LL NEED A LOT OF LEGO BRICKS, INCLUDING SOME TRAIN PARTS, BUT YOU CAN USE WHATEVER COLORS YOU WANT. IT IS PROBABLY BEST TO BE A FAIRLY EXPERIENCED LEGO BUILDER. CAN YOU TAME MY MIGHTY FIRE TRAGON?

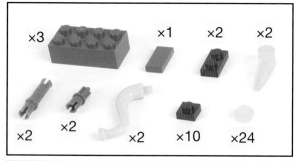

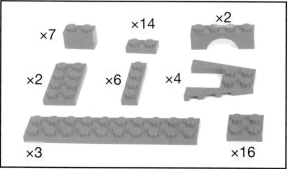

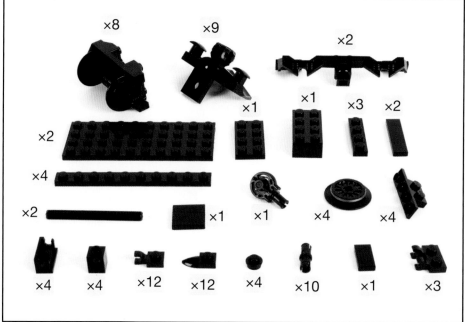

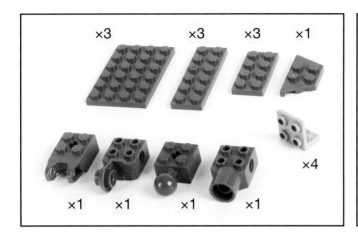

×3 ×3 ×3 ×1

×1 ×1 ×1 ×1

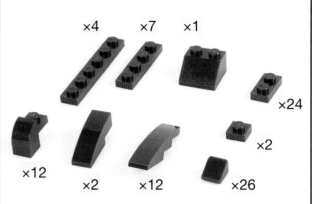

×4 ×7 ×1

×24

×2

×12 ×2 ×12 ×26

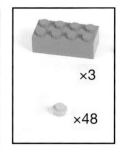

×3

×48

×14

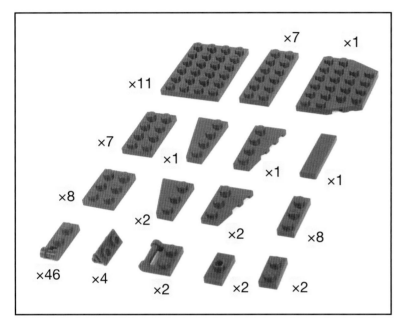

×7 ×1

×11

×7 ×1

×1 ×1

×8 ×1

×2 ×2 ×8

×46 ×4 ×2 ×2 ×2

LEGO Power Functions

Battery Box

Infrared Sensor

Train Motor

Infrared Speed
Remote Controller

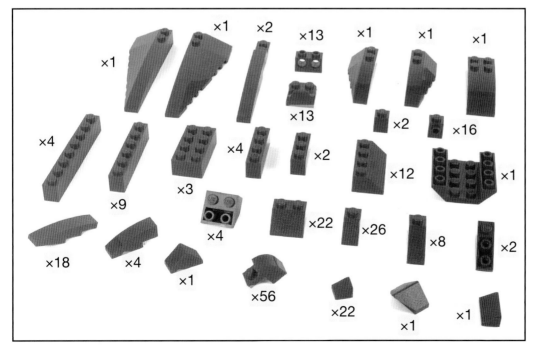

×1 ×2 ×13 ×1 ×1 ×1

×1

×13 ×2 ×16

×4 ×4 ×2

×12 ×1

×9 ×3

×4 ×22 ×26 ×8 ×2

×18 ×4 ×1

×56 ×22 ×1

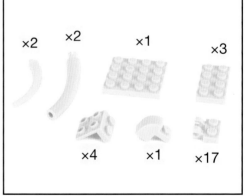

×2 ×2 ×1 ×3

×4 ×1 ×17

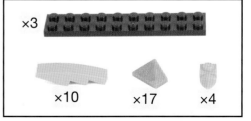

×3

×10 ×17 ×4

13

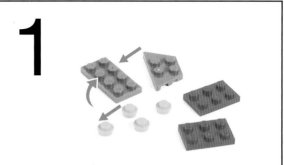

1

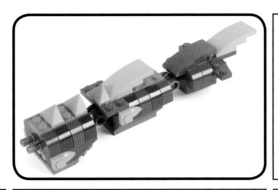

2

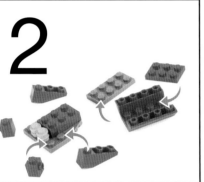

3

4

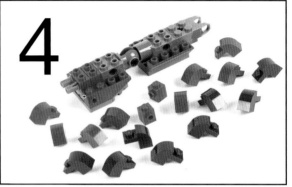

5

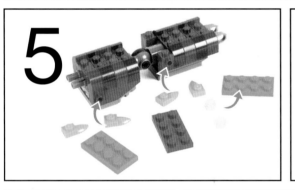

6

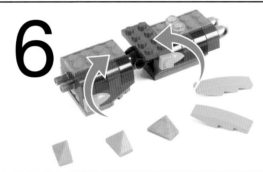

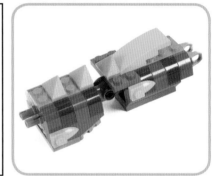

7

8

9

10

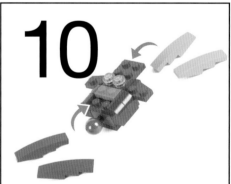

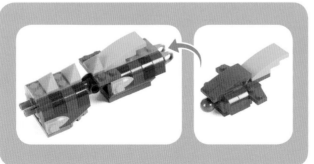

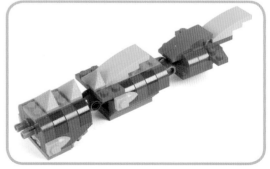

 ×3

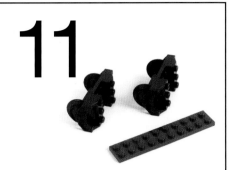 11

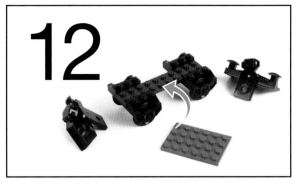 12

13

14

15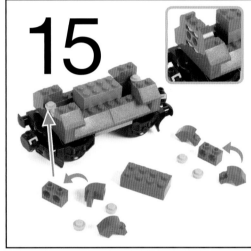

16

17

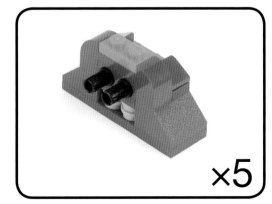 ×5

18

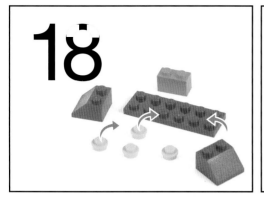

19

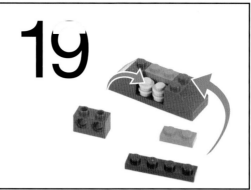

20

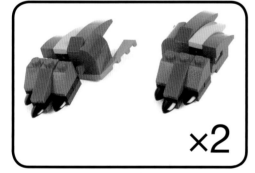

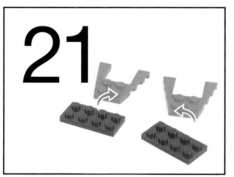

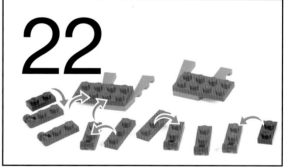

Building Tip
For some models, it's easier to build sections that snap onto a module than build them into the model.

×2

21

22

23

24

25

16

26

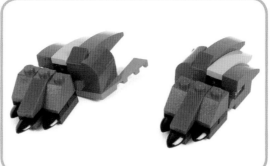

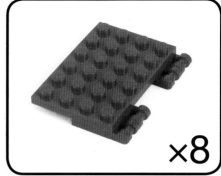

×8

27

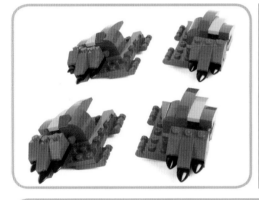
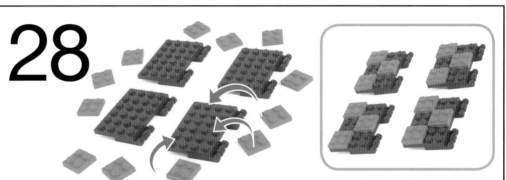

28

29

30

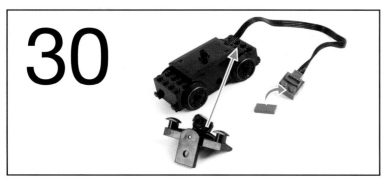

31

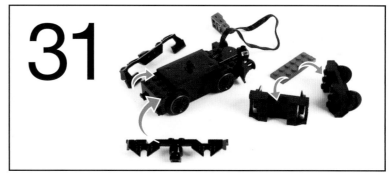

32

33

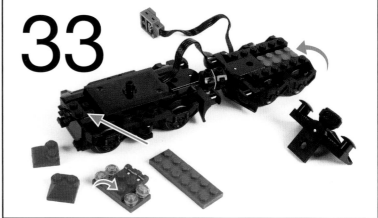

34

35

36

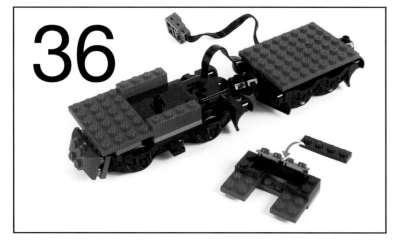

37

38

39

40

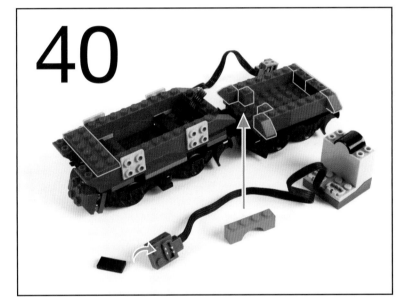

41

42

43

44

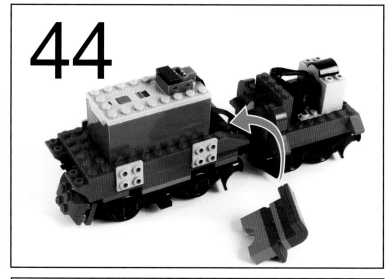

45

46

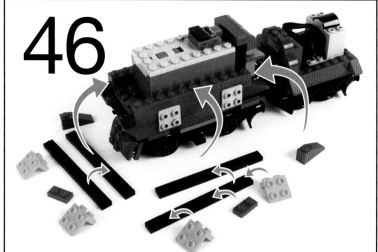

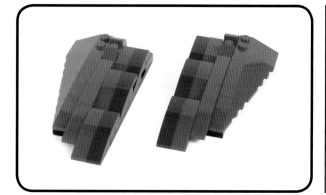

47

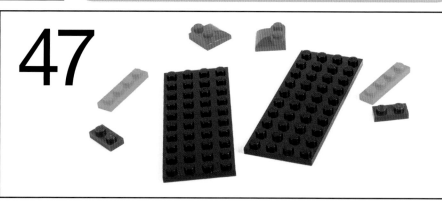

48

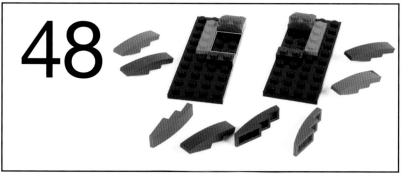

49

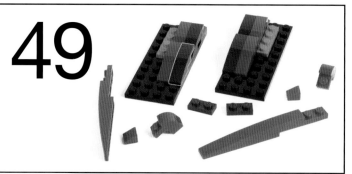

50

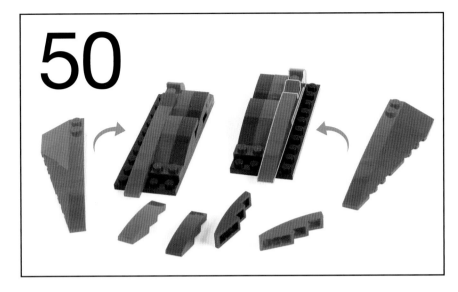

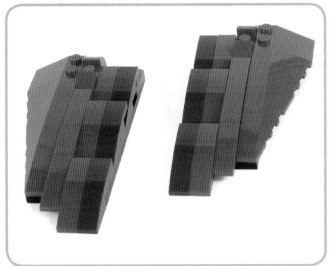

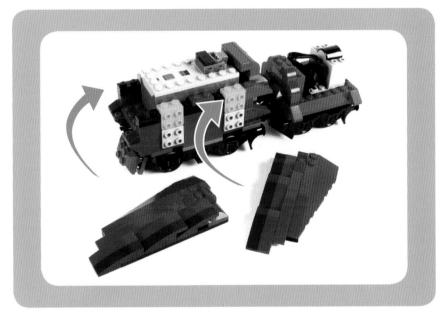

51

52

53

54

55

56
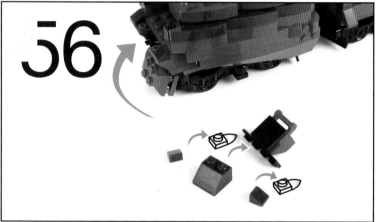

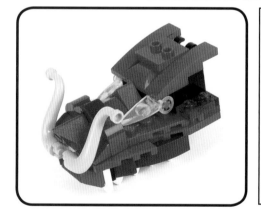

57

58

59
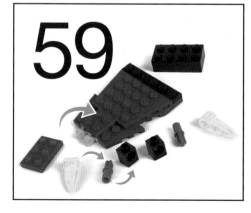

60

61

62

63

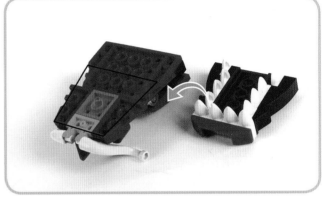

64

65

66

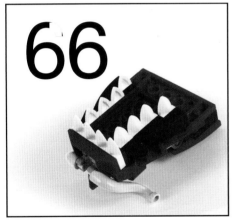

67

68

75

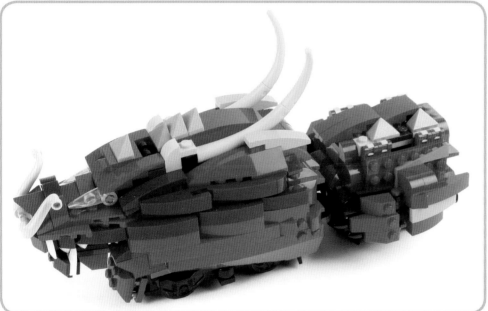

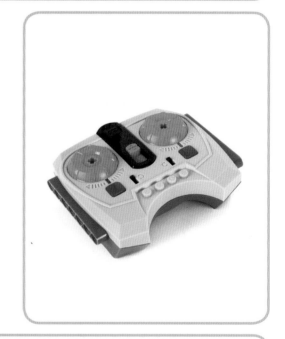

Equipment Tip
Make sure that the channel setting on the sensor matches the channel setting on your remote controller, or your tragon won't move. Also, make sure you have batteries for both the controller and the battery box in the head of your tragon.

BUILDING JOURNAL

Carl and his awesome LEGO Trains from my first adventure inspired me to build something on rails. Drawing on my passion for dragons and the versatility of LEGO Train parts, I started to build. Once I had the chassis (called a train bogie) worked out, I was able to focus on my Tragon's unique characteristics: speedy, spiky, and fiery! What type of Tragon was he going to be? Long or short claws? Fierce or friendly? I had to create smooth lines and a cool color scheme, and my Tragon was born!

The Sea Tragon

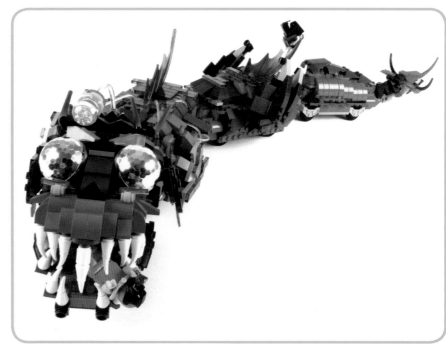

The Humboldt Tragon

THAT'S AMAZING. MIND YOU, I'M NOT SURE IT'LL FIT INTO MY SPACE BASE, BUT MAYBE I CAN USE THE TECHNIQUES TO BUILD A SPACE TRAIN!

COOL IDEA! I'LL HAVE TO HAVE TO COME BY AND CHECK IT OUT.

HEY THERE, BRICKBOT, WHAT'S GOING ON?

The last of the tests you ordered for the Transport-o-lux upgrade have finished. It is of course up to me to do all the real work and keep the place tidy.

OH, EXCELLENT. COME ON, NABII, YOU'LL LIKE THIS.

IS IT WORKING, BRICKBOT? CAN I CROSS DIMENSIONS?

TRANSDIMENSIONAL SHIFTING?! AWESOME COOLNESS!

ZOP!

UGH. WHOA, WHAT HAPPENED? BRICKBOT?

HEY, YOU'RE NOT BRICKBOT!

Silence, human! I am Badbot, and I'm in charge now!

POP!

Good to see you are both awake. I think we have a problem.

URGH. WHERE ARE MY GLASSES?

I am Badulator. Bow before me, puny humans!

ANOTHER IMPOSTER?!

POP!

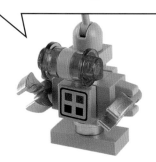

It appears we inadvertently opened a dimensional rift. After you humans passed out, a diabolical-looking figure in black appeared and shouted, "At last I am free!" Then he jumped onto the Transport-o-lux and declared, "Now to tear apart the whole universe!" and was gone in a flash!

WHAT?! HE STOLE MY RIDE?!

Affirmative, Megs, but I have tracked him. It appears there are also evil versions of me, but if I touch them, they pop back to their home dimensions.

HMMM...THAT SOUNDS LIKE A DESTRUCTOR: THE OPPOSITE OF CREATORS LIKE US. THE *COUNCIL OF CREATIVE CONSTRUCTIONISTS (TRIPLE C)* EXILED THEM ALL TO THE REALM OF BLOK MANY YEARS AGO.

OH NO! MY VIPER!

OH DEAR, YOUR SPACESHIP'S BEEN DAMAGED. LET'S SEE IF WE CAN FIX IT.

WELL, IT'S NOT SO BAD...

Silence, humans! I am—

NICE SAVE, BRICKBOT, BUT LOOK AT MY VIPER NOW!

POP!

Victorious Vipers

Mark Stafford

Nickname: Nabii

Profession: Designer

Nationality: British

Website: *www.flickr.com/photos/nabii/*

Havoc: A Viper Fighter

GET READY TO BUILD MY IMPRESSIVE STARFIGHTER! YOU SHOULDN'T HAVE TOO MUCH TROUBLE BUILDING THIS ONE.

×2 ×2 ×13 ×2

 ×1

×4 ×1 ×1
×6 ×2 ×2
×2 ×2 ×2

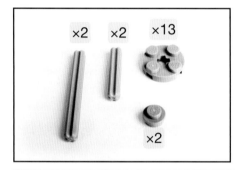
×2 ×2 ×1
×2 ×1 ×2 ×2 ×12

×12

×1

×1 ×1 ×1 ×2 ×2
×2 ×2
×2
×8 ×2 ×2
×3 ×4 ×1 ×6
×1 ×2 ×1
×2 ×12 ×8 ×2
×2 ×2 ×2 ×6
×1

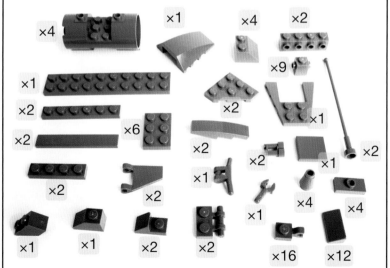
×4 ×1 ×4 ×2
×9
×1 ×2 ×1
×2 ×6 ×2
×2 ×2 ×1 ×2
×2 ×1 ×4 ×4
×1 ×1 ×2 ×2
×16 ×12

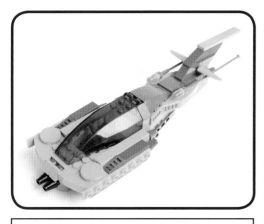

1

2
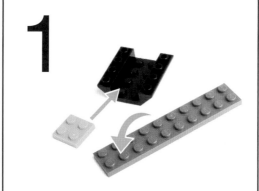

3

4

5
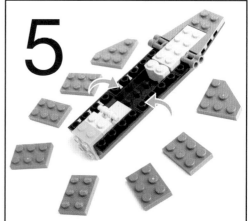

6
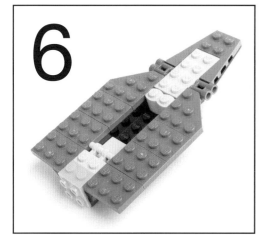

7

8
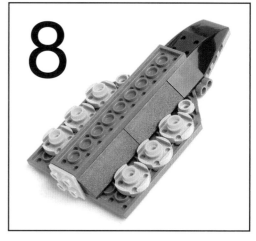

9
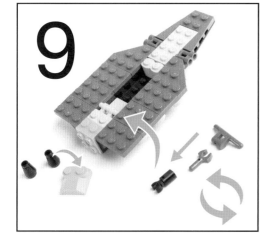

10
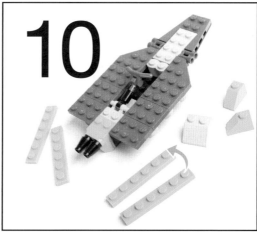

11
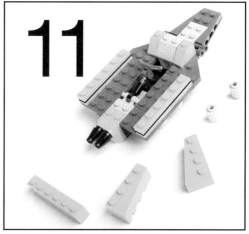

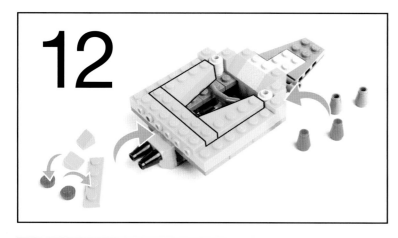

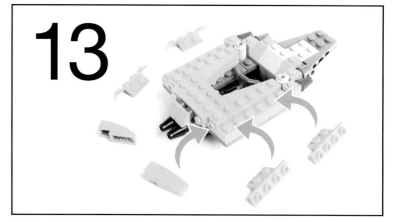

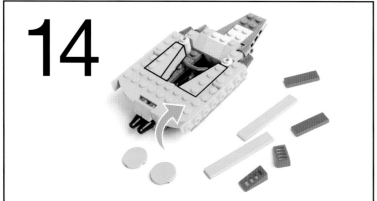

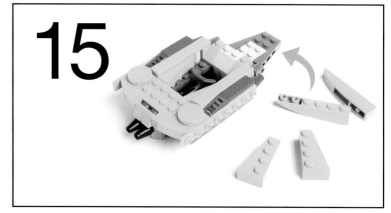

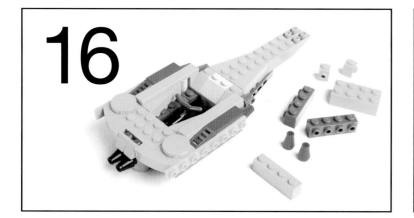

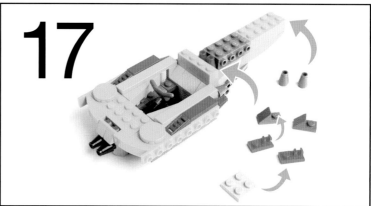

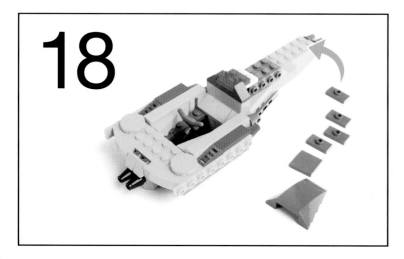

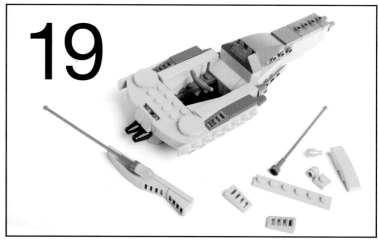

YOU NEED TO
MIRROR THIS PART
OF THE TAIL.

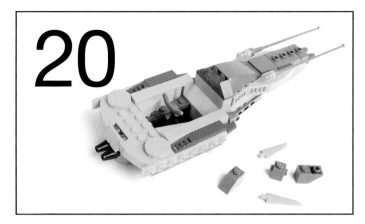

20

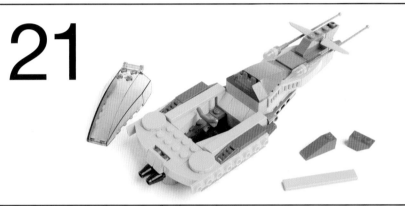

21

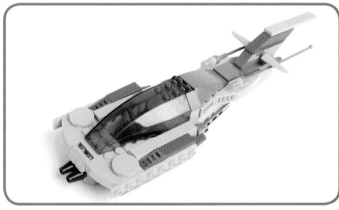

×2

22

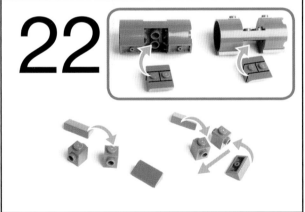

23

24

25

26

27

28

29

Building Tip
A LEGO wheel rim can also be used to design all sorts of guns and engines for a spaceship.

30

×2

31

32

33

34

35 36

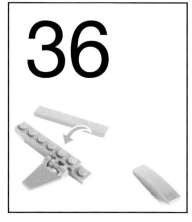

YOU NEED TO MIRROR THIS PART TOO.

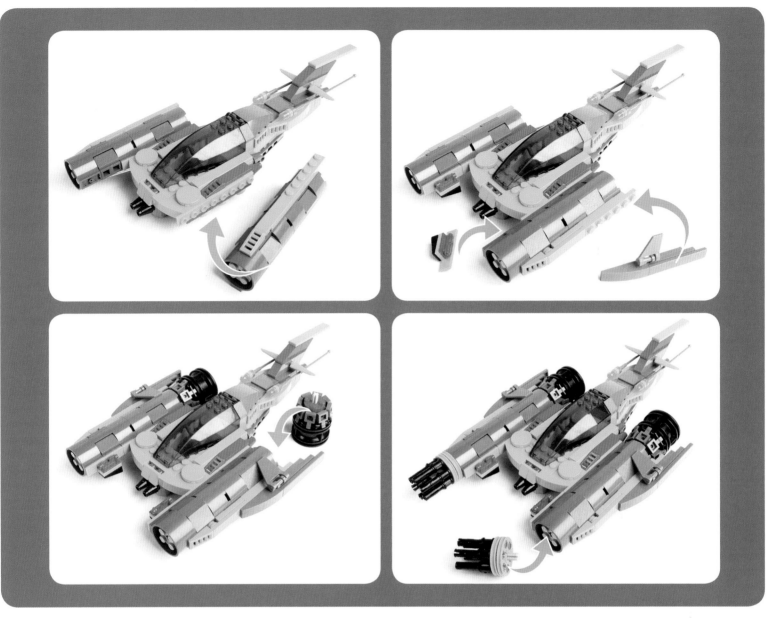

WOW, SWEET SPACESHIP! WHY'S IT CALLED A VIPER?

IT'S ACTUALLY CALLED *HAVOC*, BUT ITS FIGHTER CLASS IS VIPER. THAT'S THE NAME OF A FIGHTER SHIP FROM AN OLD COMPUTER GAME. SOME LEGO SPACE FANS STARTED AN ONLINE BUILDING CHALLENGE WITH SOME SIMPLE RULES INSPIRED BY THIS STARFIGHTER.

A LEGO Viper should have...

■ two forward prongs

■ a one-person cockpit

▥ two rear wings

■ one vertical tail fin

The rest of the build is entirely up to you.

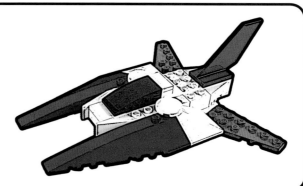

Viper Inspiration

HERE ARE JUST A FEW OF MY VIPERS. YOU SHOULD SEE MY SPACEPORT!

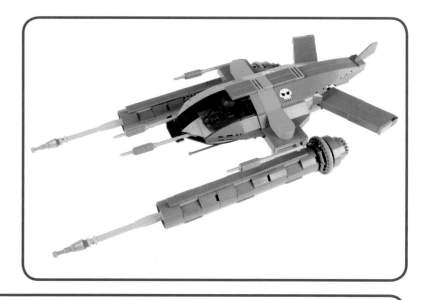

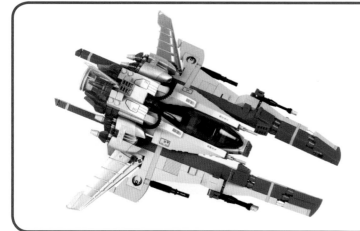

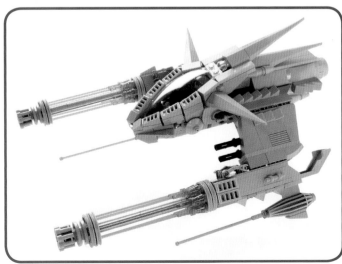

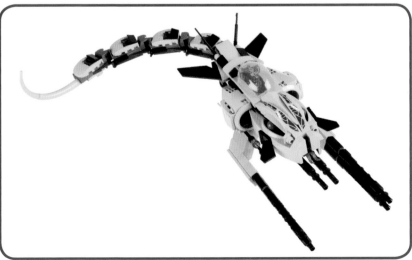

BUILDING JOURNAL

Although the release of the Destructor is still very much on my mind, I'm always open to new ideas and builds. I was intrigued by how widely Nabii had managed to take the design of his fighters while still following the Viper build rules. I think restrictions can sometimes fuel innovation and push you in unexpected directions. I'll have to remember that in my future building!

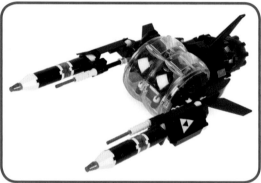

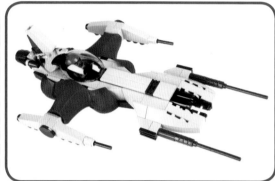

Transport-o-lux 2.0

> Megs, I have the parts for a new Transport-o-lux. I've done my part. Now it is up to you to assemble it.

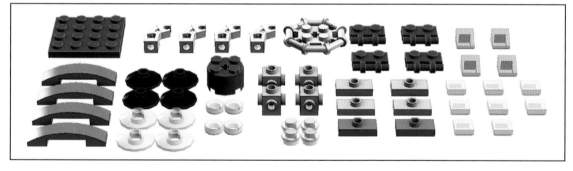

1

2

3

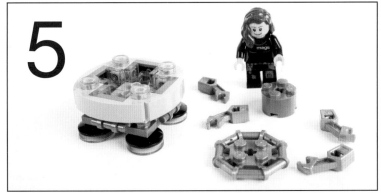

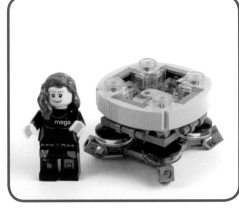

I'VE GOT A COOL NEW RIDE! NOW TO CATCH UP WITH THE DESTRUCTOR...

COOL UPGRADES! GOOD LUCK, MEGS!

SEE YOU AROUND, NABII. HAVE A SAFE JOURNEY!

PUNCH IN THE COORDINATES, BRICKBOT. I HAVE A DESTRUCTOR TO STOP!

WHOOOSH!

I SHOULD TELL THE TRIPLE C WHAT HAS HAPPENED.

OH NO! ANOTHER DESTRUCTOR!

NO, MY NAME IS MEGS. I'M A CREATOR, NOT A DESTRUCTOR. LET ME PROVE IT BY HELPING YOU UNDO ALL OF THIS DESTRUCTION!

Service with a Smile

Are J. Heiseldal

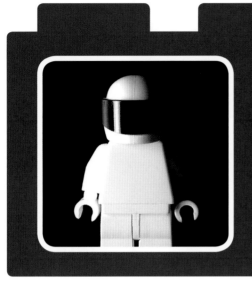

Nickname: L@go

Profession: TV Journalist

Nationality: Norwegian

Website: *www.flickr.com/photos/legolago/*

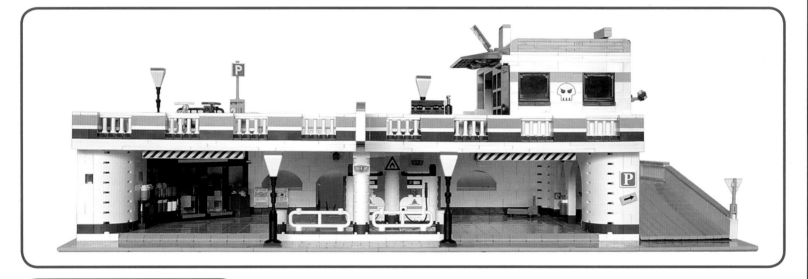

YEAH, I CAN VOUCH FOR HER, GUS. I'VE MET HER BEFORE. SHE'S FRIENDLY.

I FOUND THAT IT WAS A BIT BORING TO BE SO ANONYMOUS.

HEY, ARE! I REMEMBER YOU! YOU LOOK DIFFERENT WITHOUT YOUR HELMET ON.

GOOD FOR YOU!

Blue Eagle

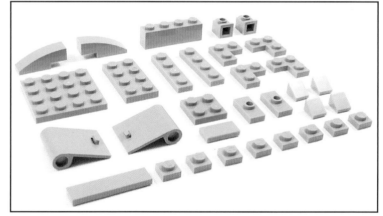

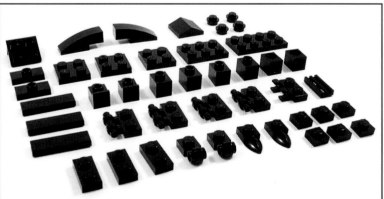

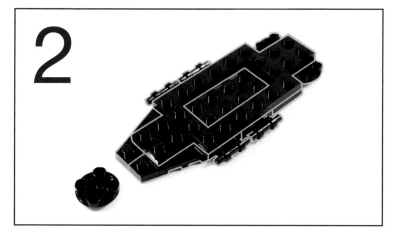

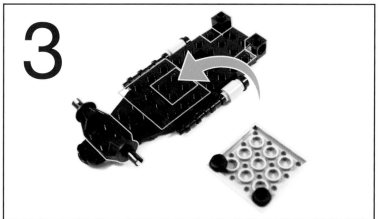

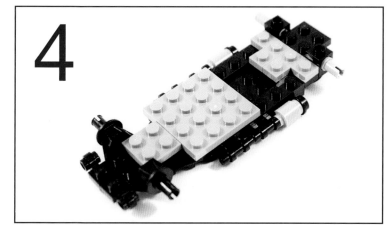

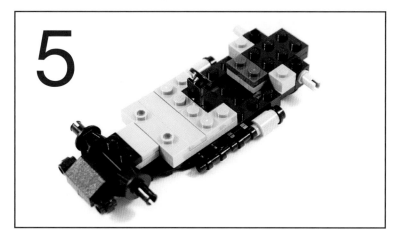

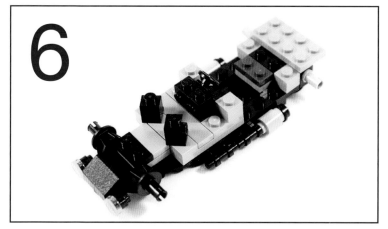

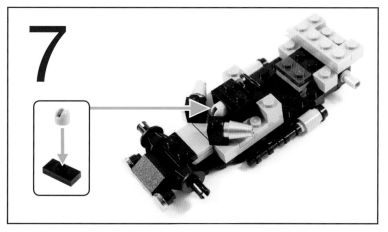

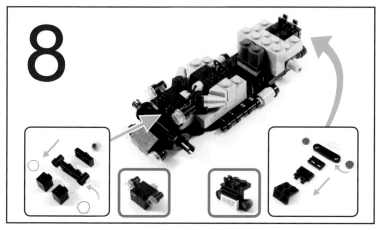

9

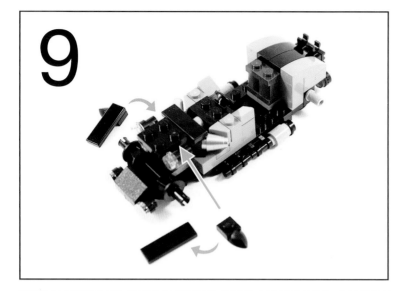

10

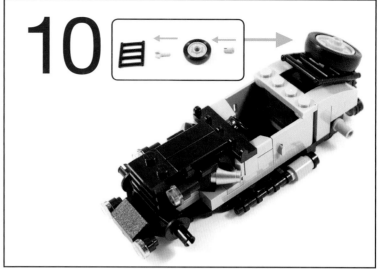

11

12

Building Tip

If you don't have these tires or this type of windscreen, you can use something similar. Use your imagination and the LEGO bricks that you have in your own collection.

HEY, YOU'VE ADDED A ROOF TO MY CONVERTIBLE! THAT'S NICE, BUT I LIKE TO FEEL THE WIND BLOWING THROUGH MY HAIR. I'LL JUST MAKE A QUICK ADJUSTMENT.

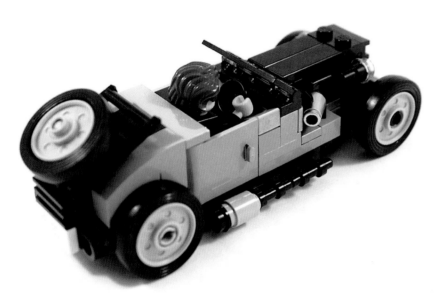

Building Tip
If you make the roof easily removable, you can turn your a car into a convertible in just a few steps. Take off the roof and add a 1×4 tile to cover the studs and create a smooth look— and voilà! You have a sleek roadster!

IT'S ACTUALLY PRETTIER THAN I REMEMBER. NOW I HAVE TO GET BACK TO MY GAS STATION BECAUSE I'M EXPECTING A GAS DELIVERY ANY MOMENT.

ARE, CAN YOU SHOW MEGS AROUND? MAYBE YOU TWO CAN CHECK TO SEE IF THE DESTRUCTOR DESTROYED ANY OTHER MODELS!

SURE THING, GUS, I'D BE HAPPY TO! MEGS, LET'S CHECK OUT GUS'S GAS STATION.

OK, THAT SOUNDS GREAT!

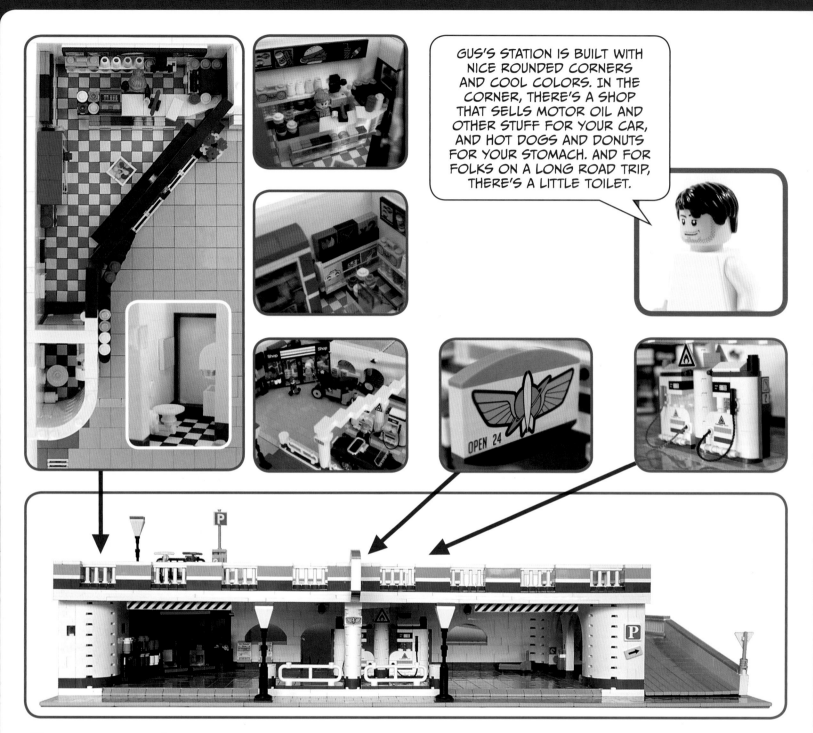

GUS'S STATION IS BUILT WITH NICE ROUNDED CORNERS AND COOL COLORS. IN THE CORNER, THERE'S A SHOP THAT SELLS MOTOR OIL AND OTHER STUFF FOR YOUR CAR, AND HOT DOGS AND DONUTS FOR YOUR STOMACH. AND FOR FOLKS ON A LONG ROAD TRIP, THERE'S A LITTLE TOILET.

Street Lamp

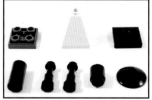

1

2

3

4

5

Gas Pump

1

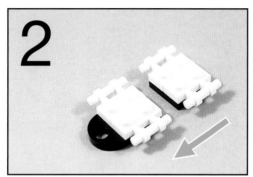
2

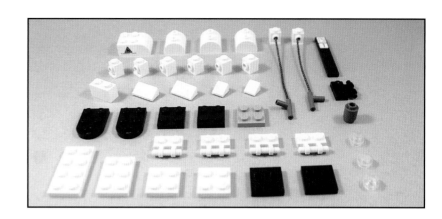
3

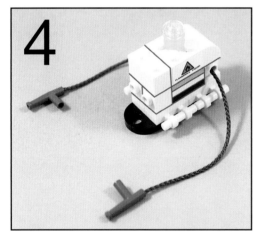
4

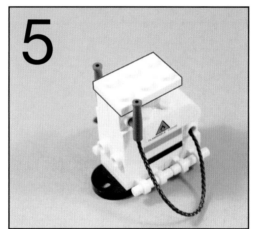
5

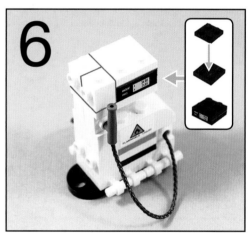
6

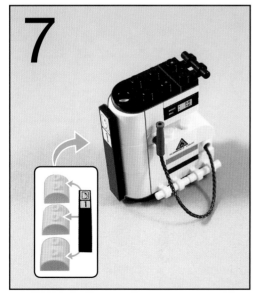
7

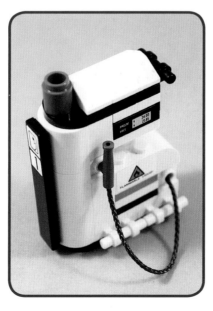

BUILDING JOURNAL

The gas station Are built for Gus has many iconic details: a corner shop, stacks of motor oil cans, a jack, tools, street lamps, and gas pumps. His use of white with light and dark blue for highlight colors creates a nice clean look. Tile elements give it a ceramic feel, and all of the details add a sense of realism to the model.

ON THE ROOF OF GUS'S GAS STATION THERE'S A BRAND-NEW CLUBHOUSE FOR THE LOCAL HOT ROD CLUB, WHICH OUTGREW ITS OLD HANGOUT FROM 1994. IT'S THE PLACE TO BE IF YOU'RE CRAZY ABOUT COOL RIDES AND MEAN MACHINES, WITH PLENTY OF PARKING SPACES OUTSIDE FOR THE CLUB MEMBERS—OR ANYBODY ELSE WHO WANTS TO CHECK OUT WHAT'S GOING ON.

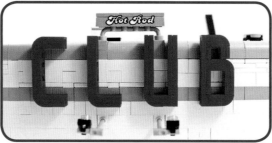

Lawn Chair

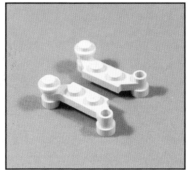
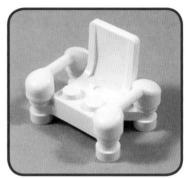

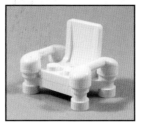
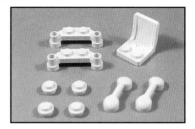

BBQ

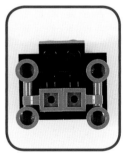

BUILDING JOURNAL

The Hot Rod Club is a perfect hangout for hot-rodders! Building a BBQ grill and a picnic table helps to tie everything together. A sofa, TV, and car parts on the wall say right away this is a place for car fans. I should remember to think of some iconic details that suit the character of the building for the next time I build an interior.

Clubhouse Sofa

THIS IS THE PERFECT PLACE TO CHILL OUT AFTER WORKING ON CARS ALL DAY.

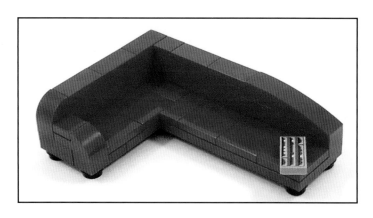

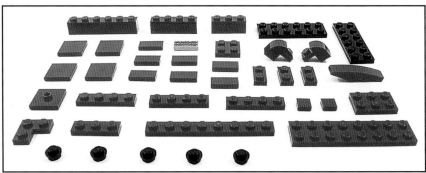

1

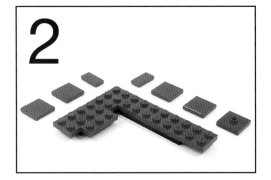

2

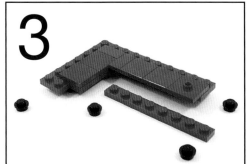

3

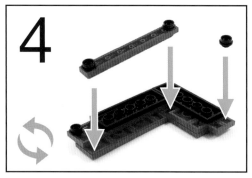

4

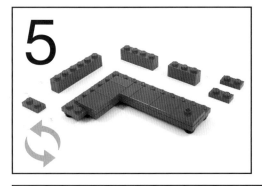

5

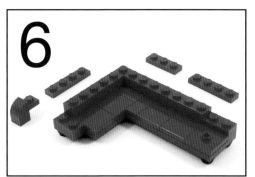

6

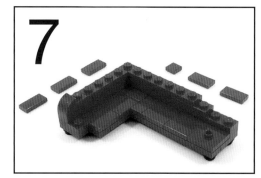

7

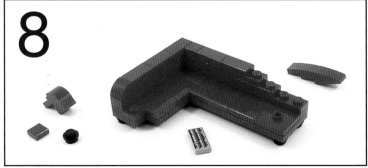

8

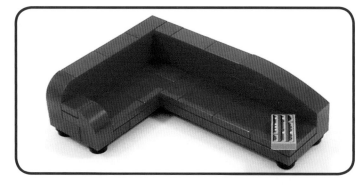

THERE'S A RAMP THAT GOES AROUND THE BACK SO THAT THE HOT RODS CAN GET UP TO THE CLUBHOUSE. OH! I'M SURE THAT IF GUS HAD KNOWN WE WERE COMING, HE'D HAVE REMOVED THAT GARBAGE PILE BEHIND THE GAS STATION! I'M SORRY ABOUT THAT.

Water Fountain

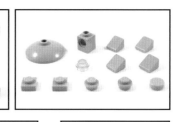

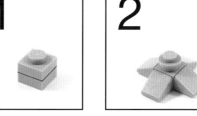

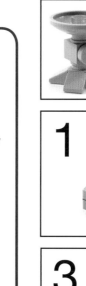

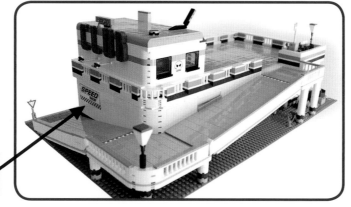

Building Tip
Including stickers that complement your model is a great way to add character to your build.

Building Tip
You can make a gas station more realistic by adding details like a drinking fountain and some old boxes lying around. Try using some old, dirty bricks as garbage—and maybe even add a rat looking for a snack!

Hot Howler

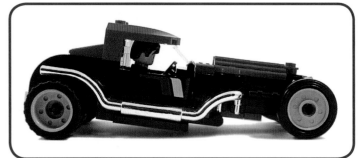

Sweet Yello

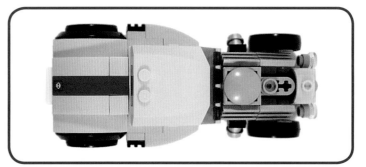

Rebel Roadster

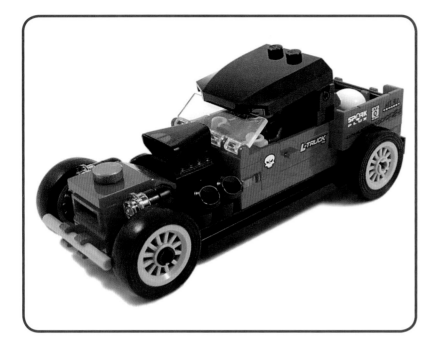

THE MEMBERS OF THE HOT ROD CLUB OFTEN GIVE THEIR CARS NAMES THAT SOUND ANGRY OR DANGEROUS. BUT UNDERNEATH THAT TOUGH IMAGE, THEY'RE REALLY FRIENDLY GUYS!

Building Tip
Hot rods and muscle cars often have a wide rear axle and bigger rear wheels to give them an aggressive and fast look. If you don't have wheels in different sizes, you can change the axle width by placing the rear wheels farther apart than the front wheels.

Gas Guzzler

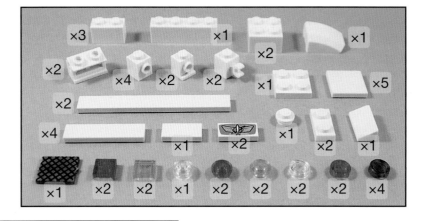

Building Tip
These light and dark blue colors might not be very common, but you can always build your truck using other colors. If you don't have the large, curved elements, try building a container for the back of your truck.

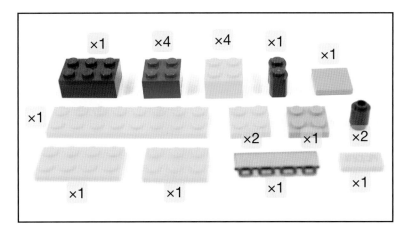

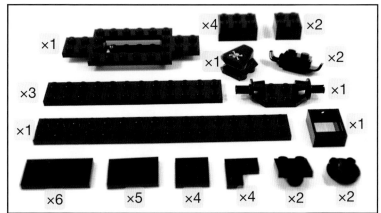

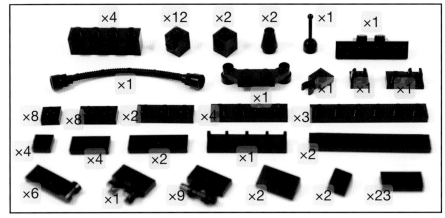

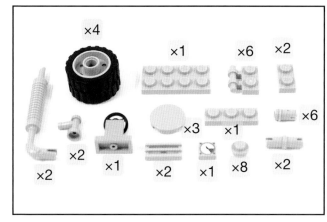

YOU NEED TO BUILD THE GUZZLER IN THREE PARTS, STARTING WITH THE CAB. EVERY VEHICLE STARTS WITH A CHASSIS. THIS ONE IS A BIT TRICKY, SO PAY ATTENTION TO THE SUBASSEMBLIES!

1

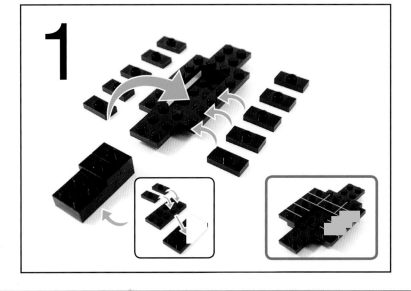

2

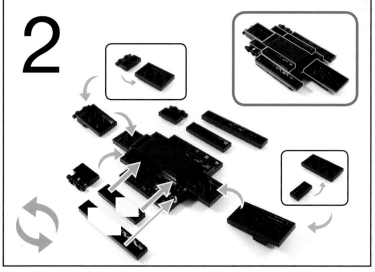

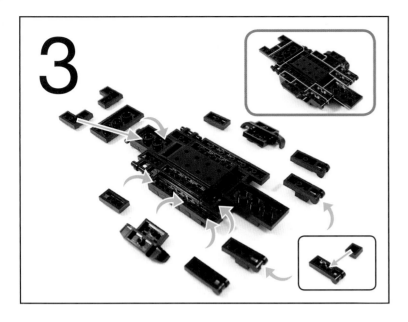

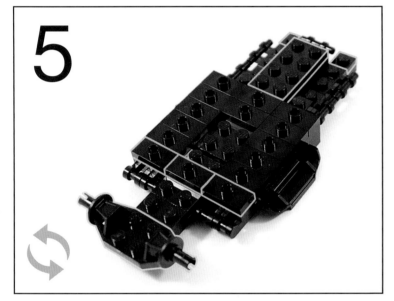

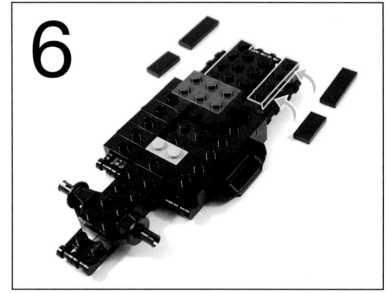

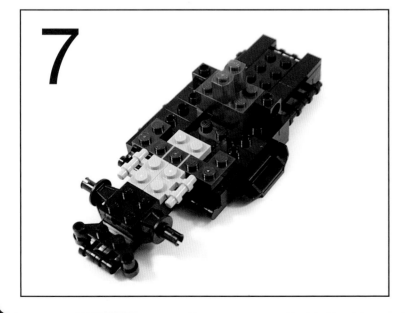

9

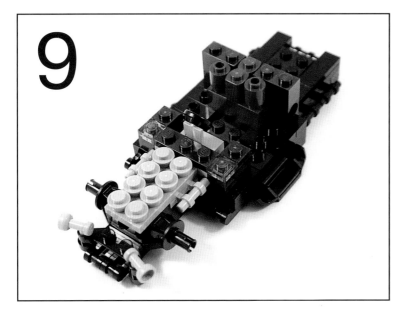

10

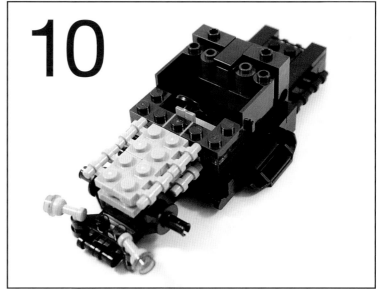

11

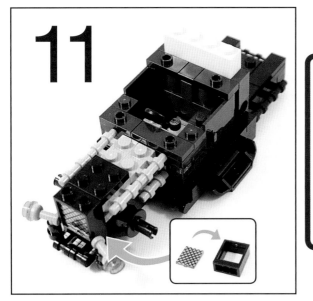

Building Tip
Try combining stickers of different patterns and opacity for unusual and cool effects. Don't be afraid to experiment. This grille was made from a mirror sticker with a transparent mesh sticker on top, placed on a piece of window glass.

12

13

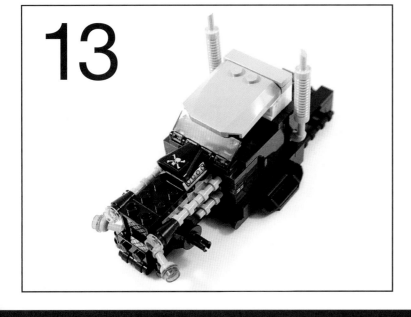

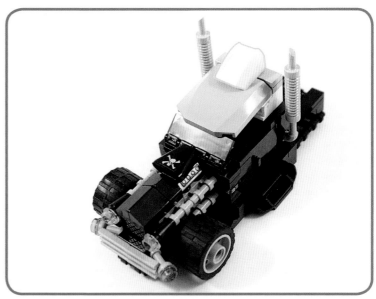

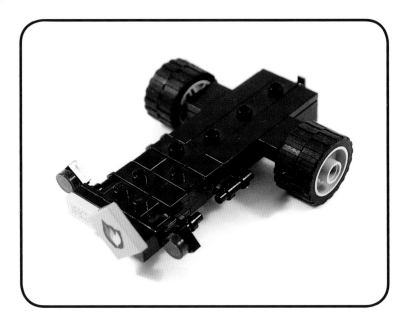

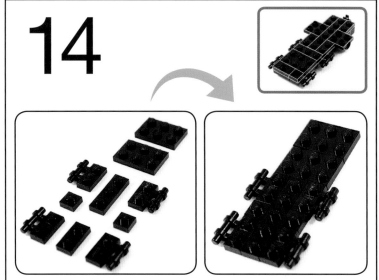

14

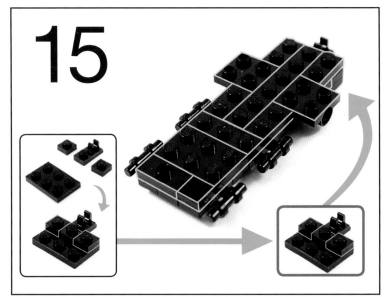

15

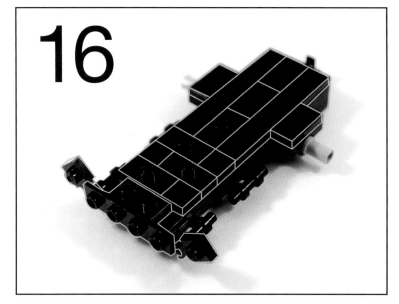

16

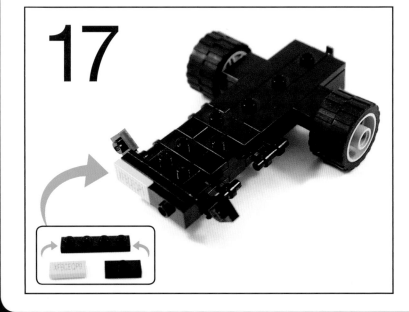

17

CLICK

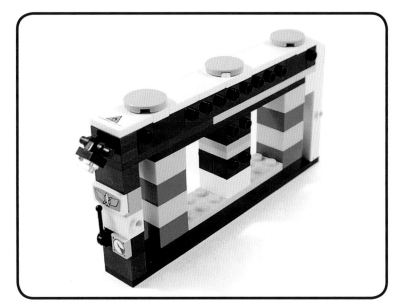

18

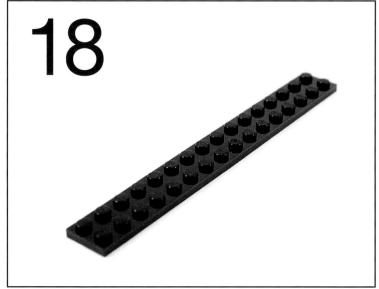

19

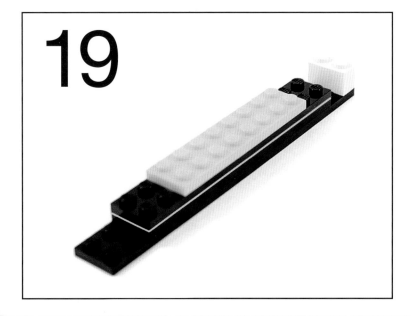

20

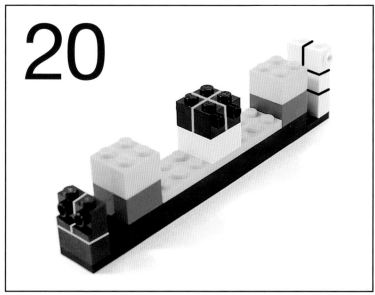

21

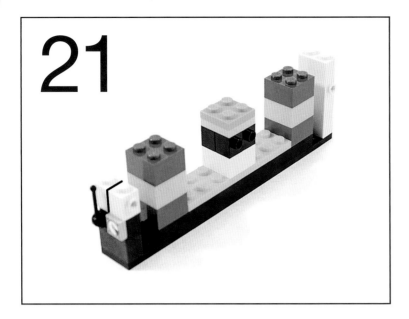

22

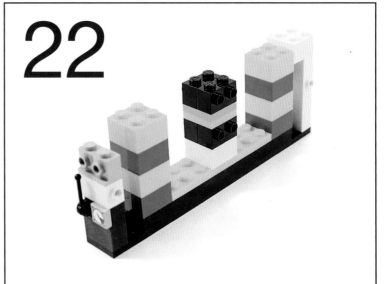

23

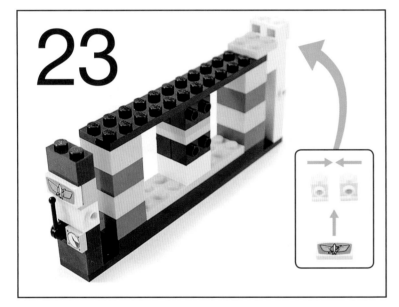

24

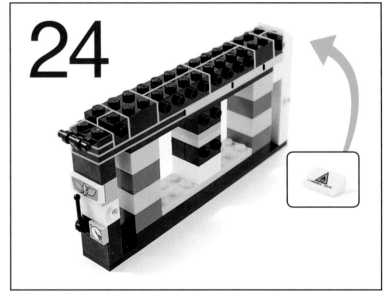

25

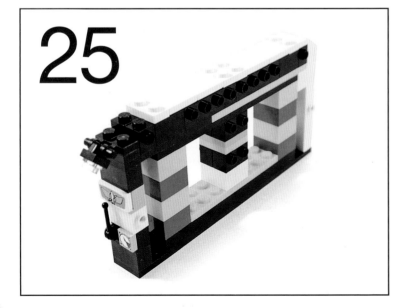

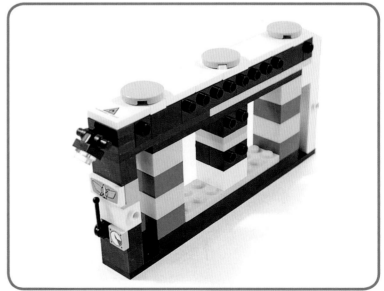

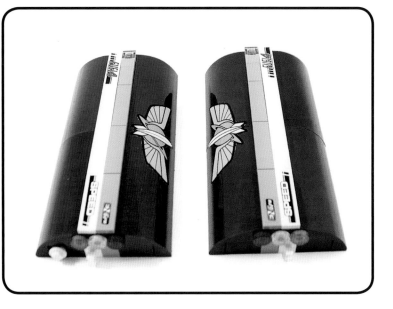

26

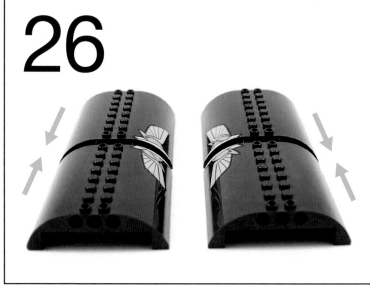

27

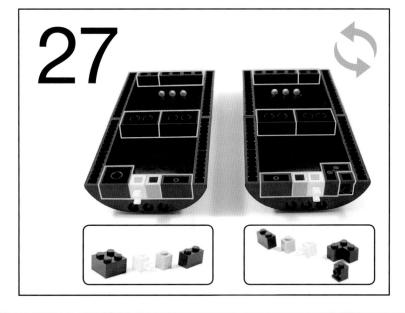

28

29

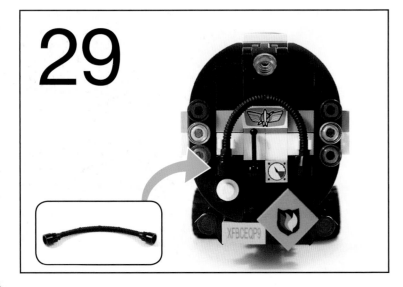

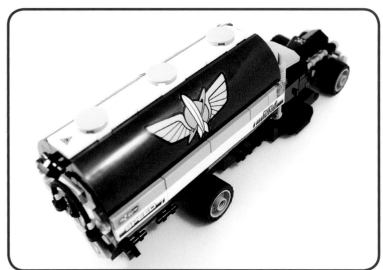

BUILDING JOURNAL

Are has built his tanker truck with a lot of iconic details that you would find in a real one: a long wheel base, a beefy body, smoke stacks, and a large fuel tank with a hazardous materials symbol on its rear bumper. He's combined these traditional elements with some details you'd find on a hot rod: a supercharged, exposed engine and a sleek nose. This cool idea gives the impression of speed. Maybe I should soup up my Idea Truck, too!

HEY! WHAT ARE YOU DOING TO MY TRUCK! THAT'S NOT HOW IT'S SUPPOSED TO LOOK!

THE WHAT?

SORRY! WE JUST REBUILT IT AFTER IT GOT DESTROYED BY THE DESTRUCTOR.

THE DESTRUCTOR. I ACCIDENTALLY FREED HIM, AND NOW HE'S—

I DON'T HAVE TIME FOR THIS. I HAVE GAS TO DELIVER!

COUGH

COUGH

VROOOMMM!

WELL, SO MUCH FOR BEING HELPFUL...

YEAH, I KNOW, RIGHT?

AAARRRRGHHHH!!!

WHAT ON EARTH WAS THAT?

I DON'T KNOW, BUT I SUSPECT THE DESTRUCTOR HAD SOMETHING TO DO WITH IT. WELL, EVERYTHING SEEMS TO BE FINE HERE NOW, SO I'M GOING TO GO CHECK IT OUT!

GOOD LUCK, MEGS, AND BE CAREFUL! MAYBE YOU COULD HITCH A RIDE WITH THAT GUY. HE SEEMS TO BE HEADED THAT WAY, TOO.

I WILL! THANKS FOR THE TOUR, ARE. SEE YOU AROUND!

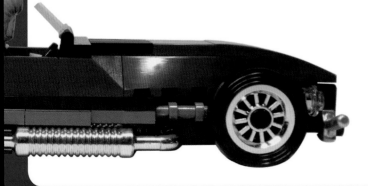

A Ferry Nice Build

Arjan Oude Kotte

Nickname: Konajra

Profession: Bicycle Mechanic

Nationality: Dutch

Websites: *www.konajra.com/*
www.flickr.com/photos/konajra/sets/

Car Ferry

IF YOU WISH TO BUILD MY FERRY, YOU'LL NEED TO PUT ON YOUR ENGINEER'S THINKING CAP. I WOULD RECOMMEND THIS MODEL FOR AN INTERMEDIATE BUILDER. GOOD LUCK!

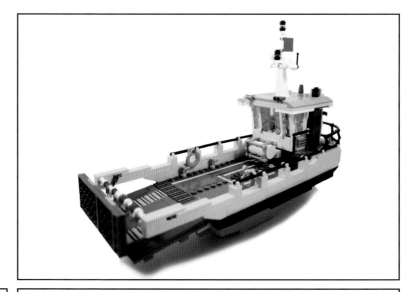

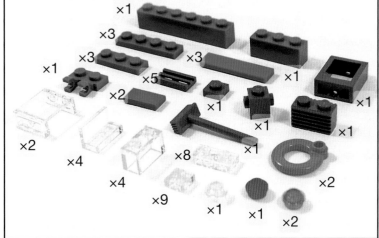

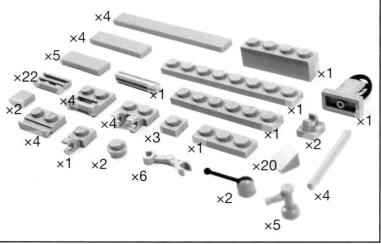

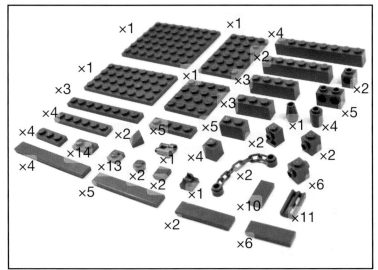

×1 ×1 ×4 ×2 ×1 ×3 ×3 ×2 ×3 ×4 ×5 ×2 ×5 ×5 ×1 ×4 ×4 ×14 ×2 ×1 ×4 ×2 ×4 ×13 ×2 ×2 ×5 ×1 ×6 ×2 ×10 ×11 ×2 ×6

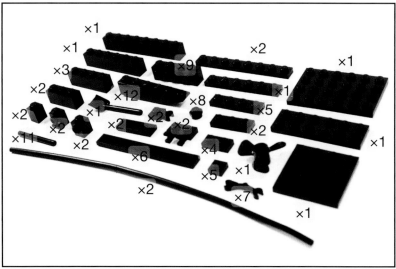

×1 ×1 ×2 ×1 ×9 ×3 ×2 ×1 ×2 ×12 ×8 ×5 ×2 ×2 ×2 ×2 ×2 ×11 ×2 ×6 ×4 ×5 ×1 ×2 ×7 ×1

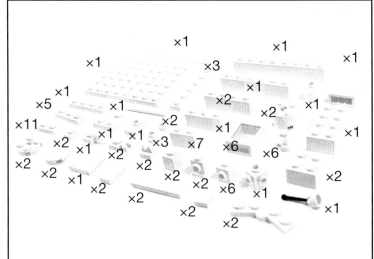

×1 ×1 ×1 ×1 ×3 ×5 ×1 ×1 ×11 ×1 ×1 ×2 ×2 ×1 ×3 ×7 ×6 ×6 ×2 ×1 ×2 ×1 ×3 ×2 ×2 ×1 ×2 ×2 ×6 ×1 ×2 ×1 ×2 ×2

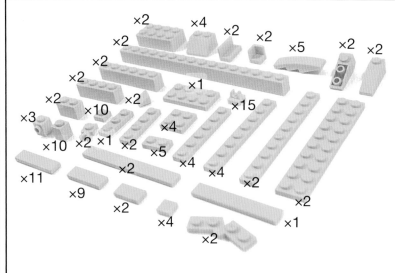

×2 ×4 ×2 ×2 ×2 ×5 ×2 ×2 ×2 ×2 ×1 ×15 ×2 ×10 ×4 ×3 ×10 ×2 ×1 ×2 ×5 ×4 ×11 ×2 ×4 ×9 ×2 ×2 ×2 ×4 ×2 ×1

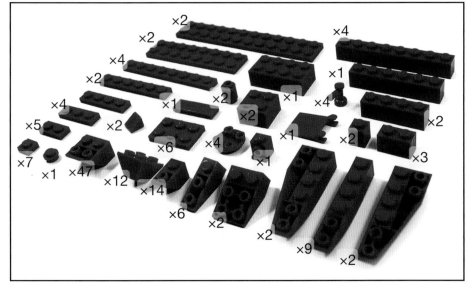

×2 ×4 ×2 ×4 ×1 ×2 ×4 ×2 ×1 ×1 ×5 ×2 ×2 ×2 ×1 ×6 ×4 ×2 ×3 ×7 ×1 ×47 ×12 ×14 ×6 ×2 ×2 ×9 ×2

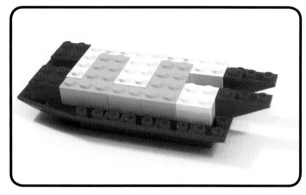

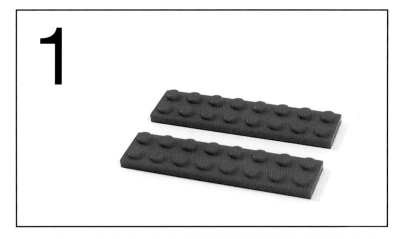

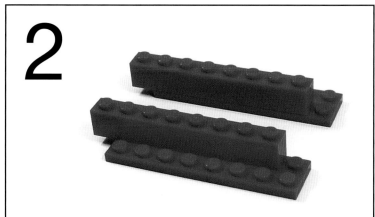

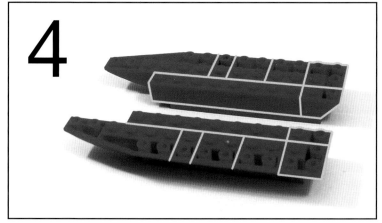

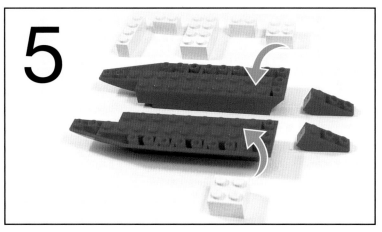

Building Tip
Alternating slopes by one stud on each layer helps to lock the layer below. This increases stability and makes for a better build. This technique works for both inverse slopes like these and for regular slopes such as that of a roof top.

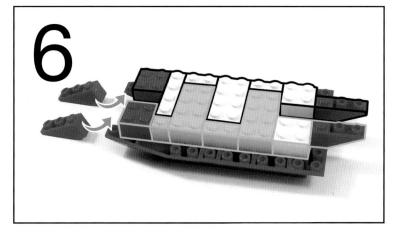

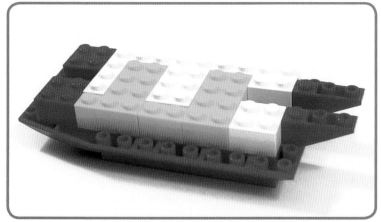

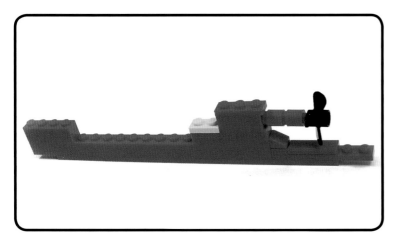

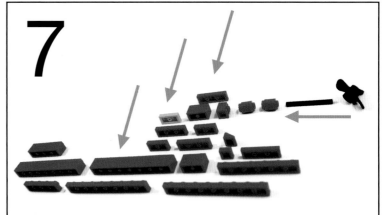

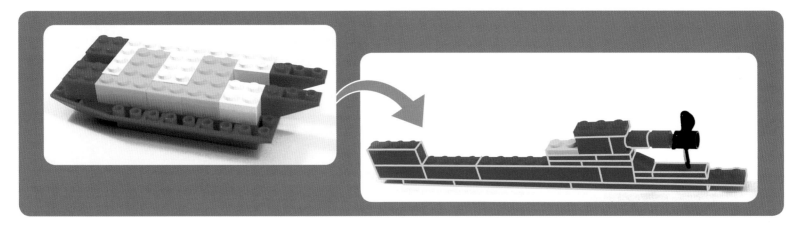

8

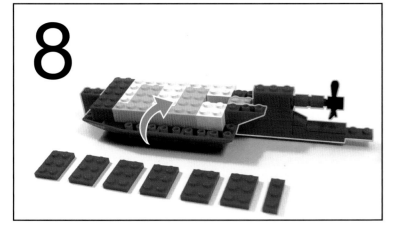

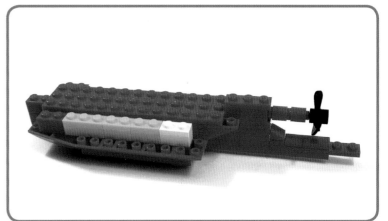

9

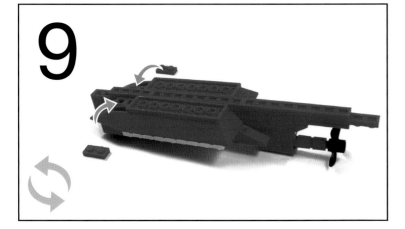

10

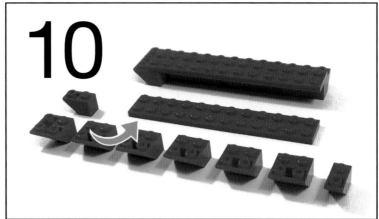

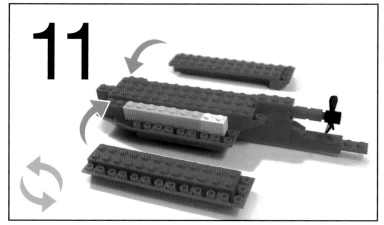

11

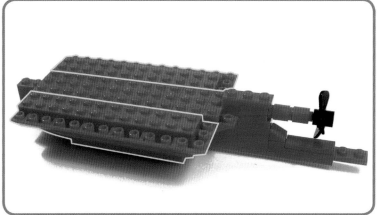

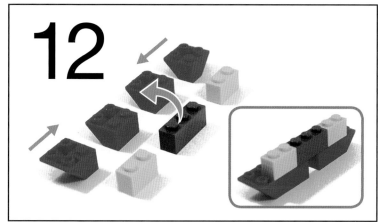

12

13

14

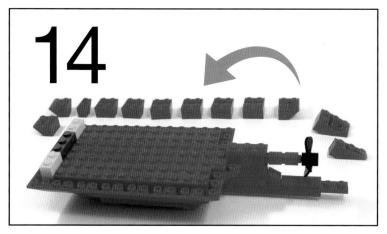

15

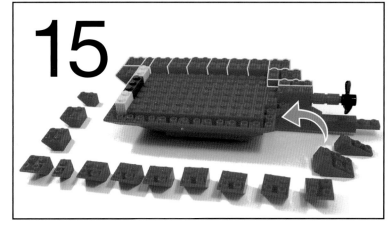

16

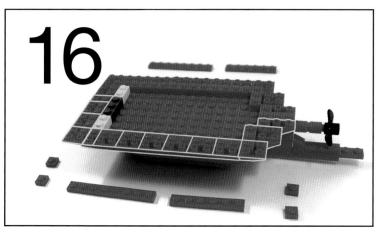

17

×2

18

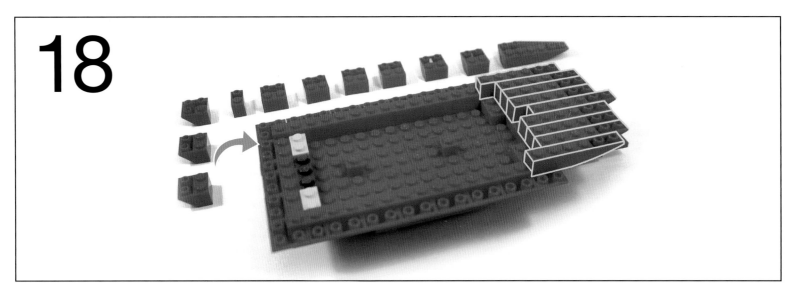

19

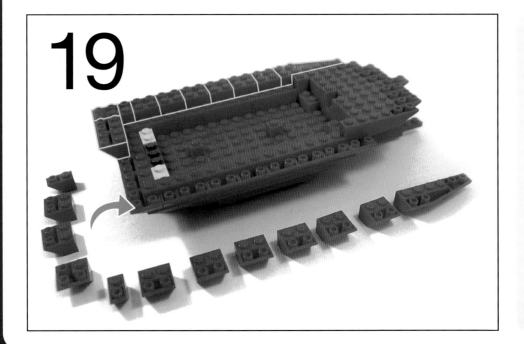

BUILDING JOURNAL

Arjan and I talked a lot as we rebuilt his ferry. He told me he likes to put lots of details into every model at the beginning of the build. That way, he can tell if it will turn out the way he wants. Most of his LEGO models are quite large, but they are all minifigure scale and have a lot of functions that are found on a real vessel. I think his models are incredible!

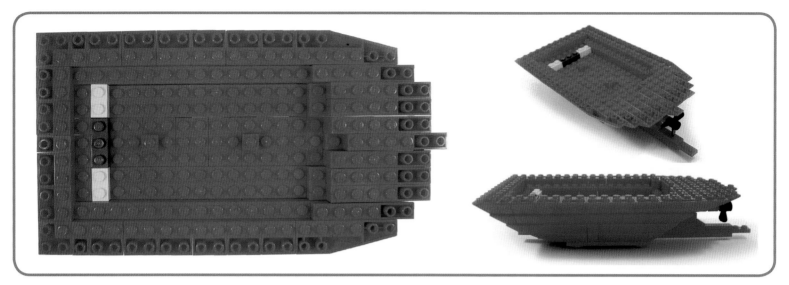

20

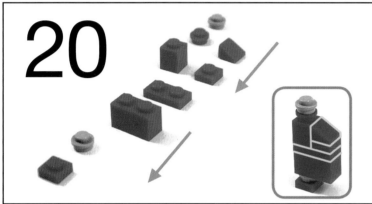

21

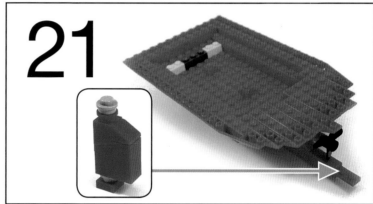

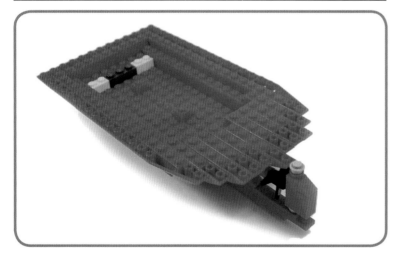

22

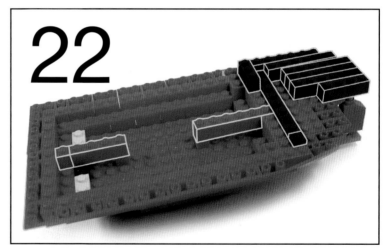

BUILDING JOURNAL

Arjan is partial to industrial machines, like ships used for fishing or transportation, that will get dirty, beaten up, and rusty. He often builds replica models, using references images from the Internet. When he finds something he wants to build, he looks for detailed plans or technical drawings so he can re-create it at a 1:40 scale.

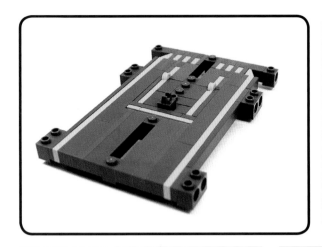

23

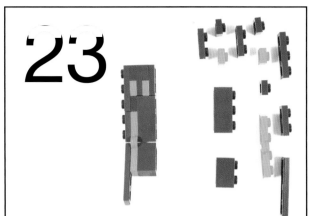

24

25

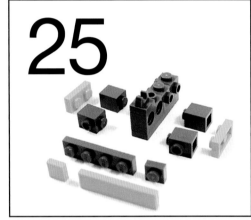

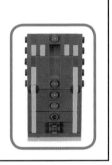

26

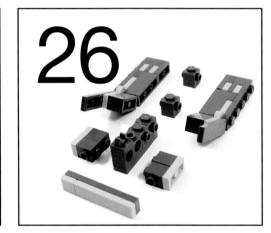

27

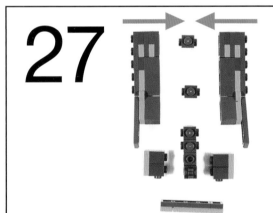

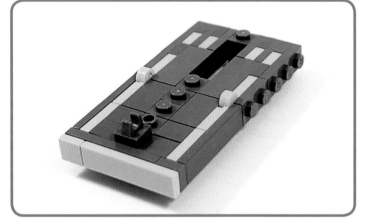

28

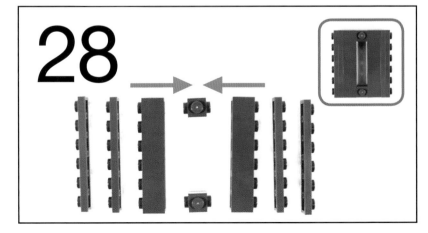

29

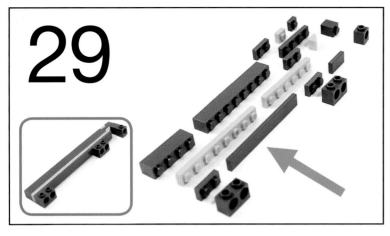

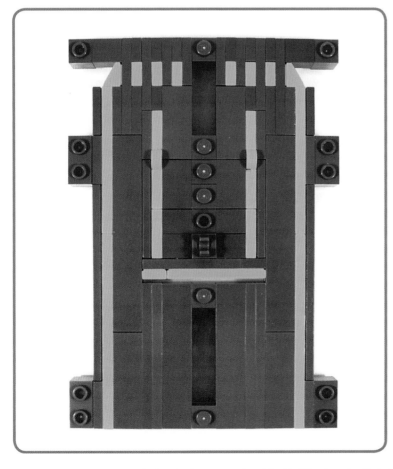

30

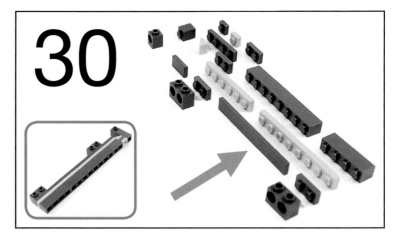

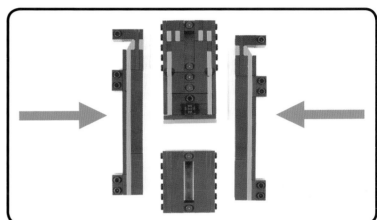

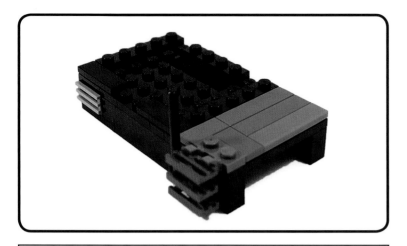

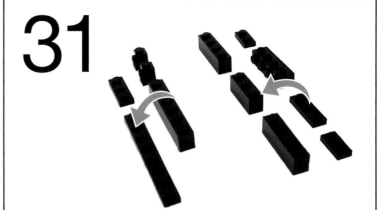

31

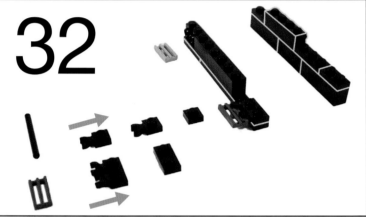

32

33

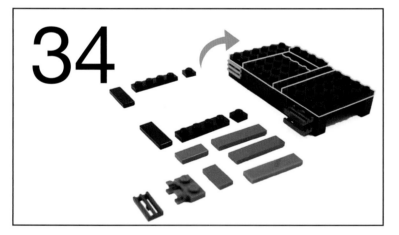

34

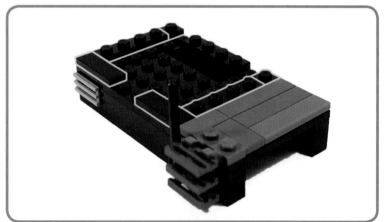

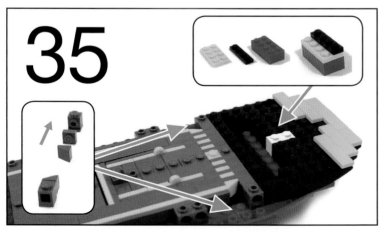

35

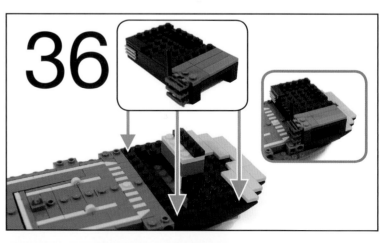

36

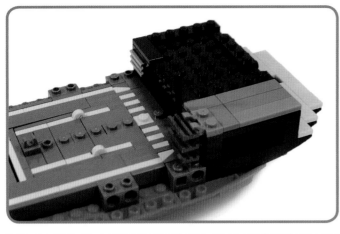

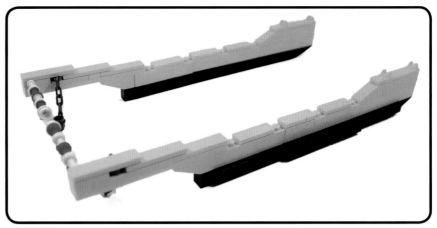

37

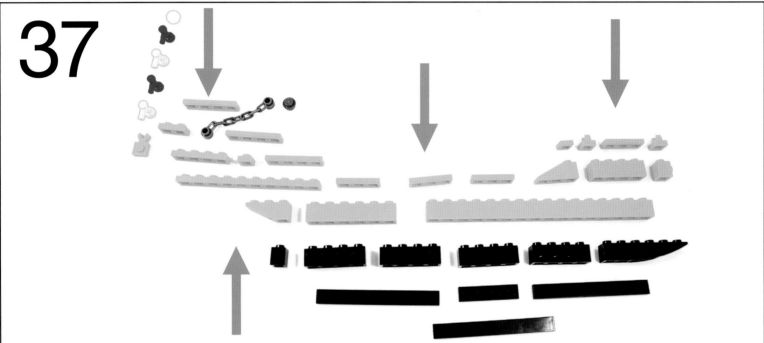

YOU WILL NEED TO BUILD TWO SIDE RAILS. JUST MIRROR THESE STEPS.

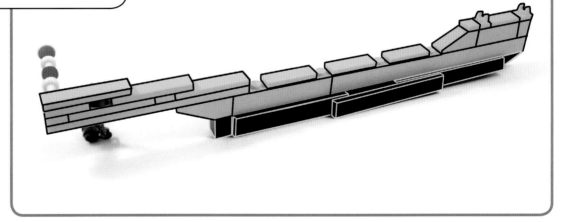

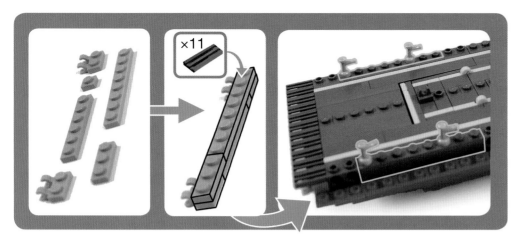

×11

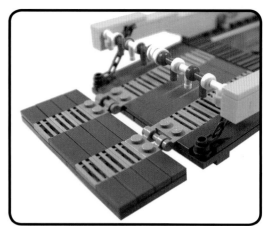

38

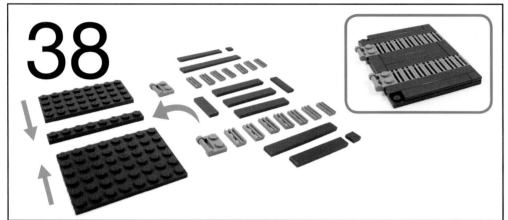

39

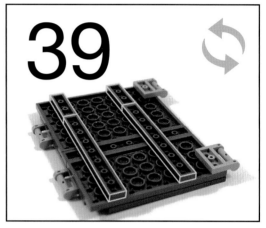

40

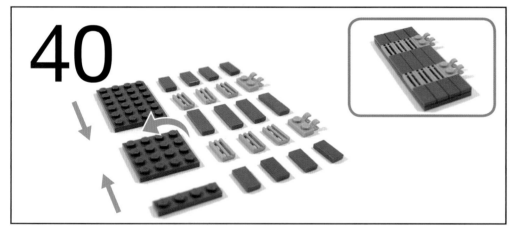

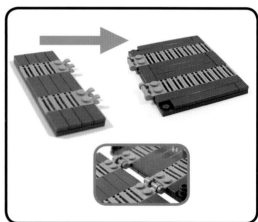

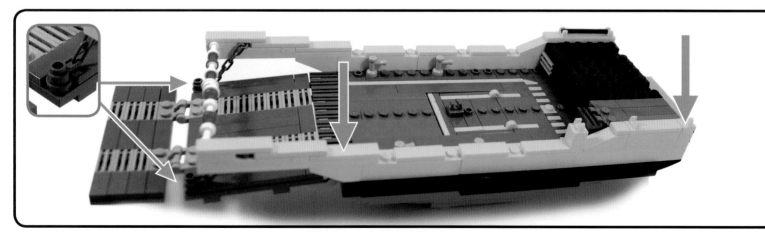

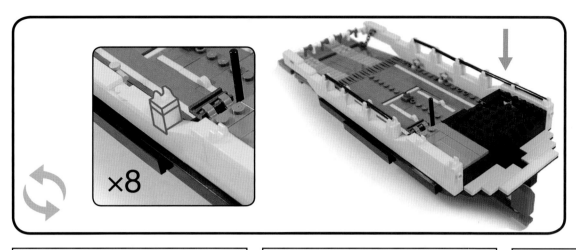

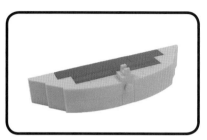

41

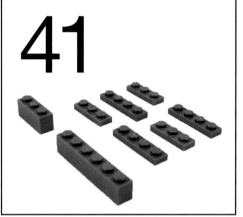

42

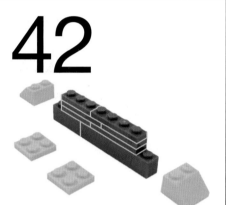

43

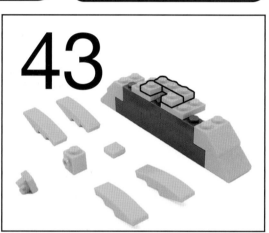

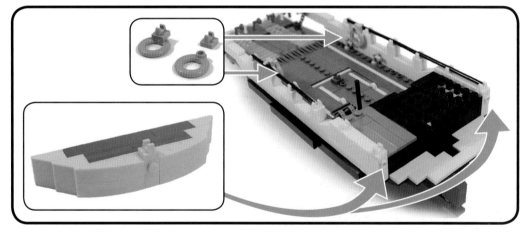

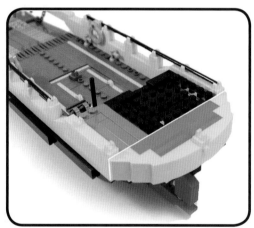

44

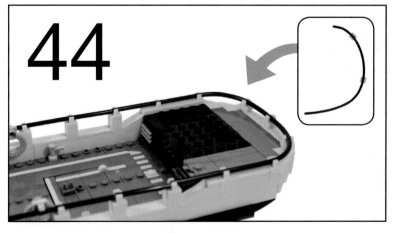

45

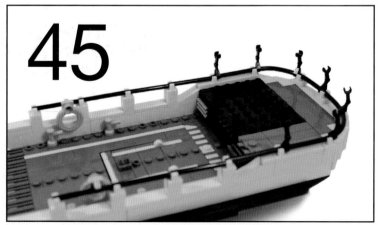

46

47

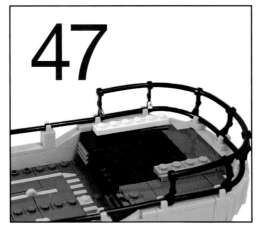

48

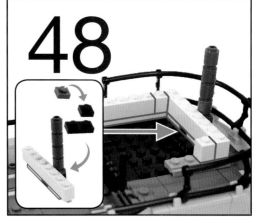

49

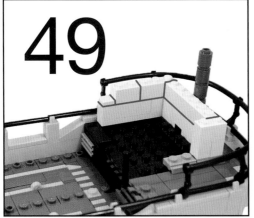

50

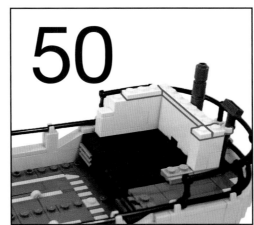

51

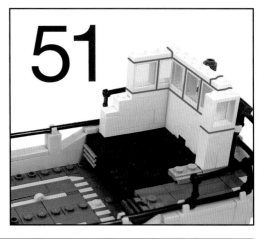

52

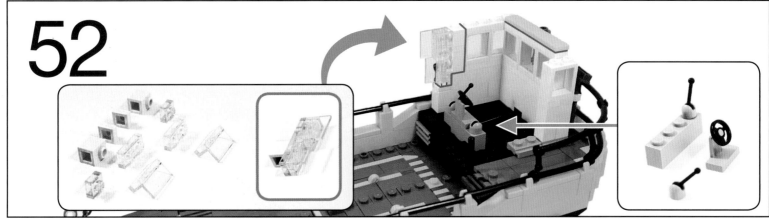

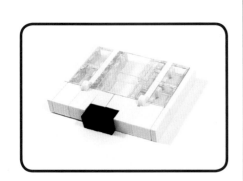

53

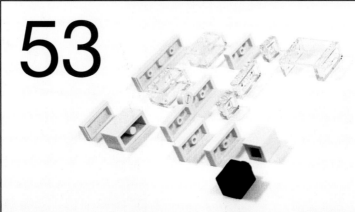

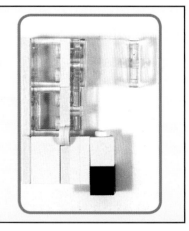

54

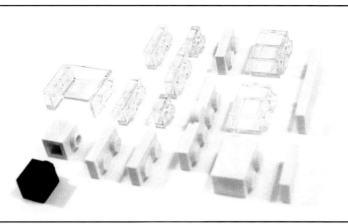

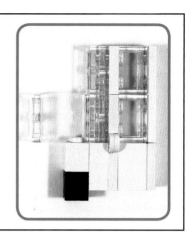

55

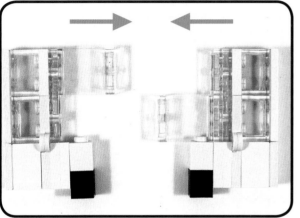

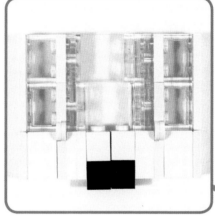

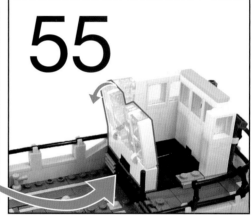

56

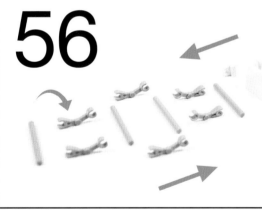

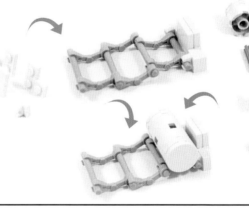

57

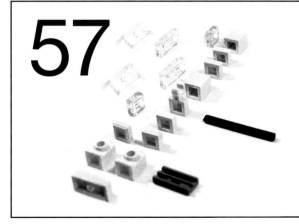

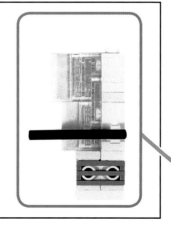

58

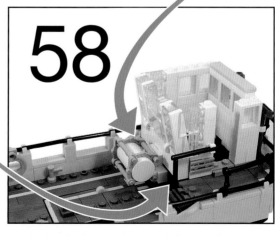

59

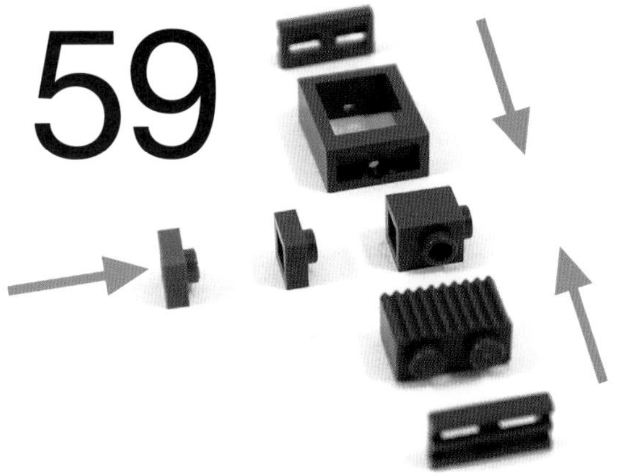

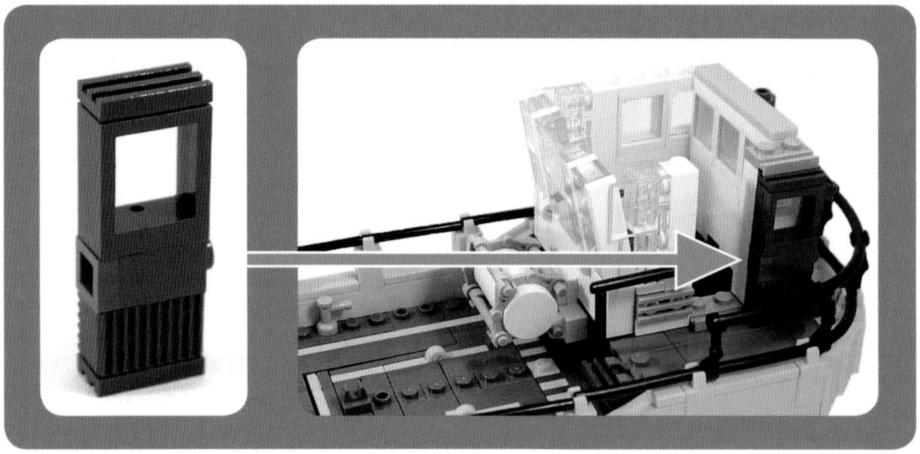

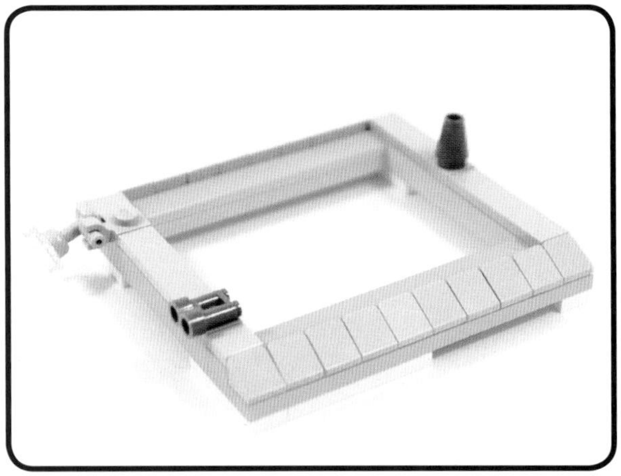

60

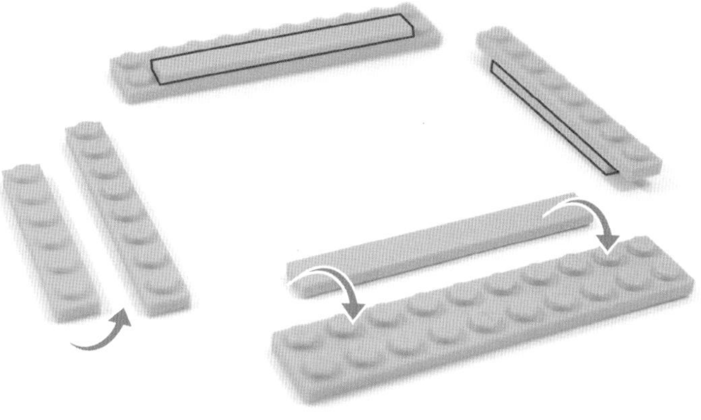

61

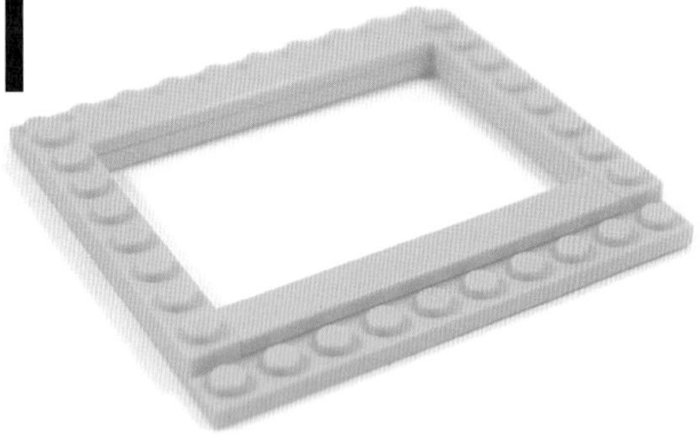

62

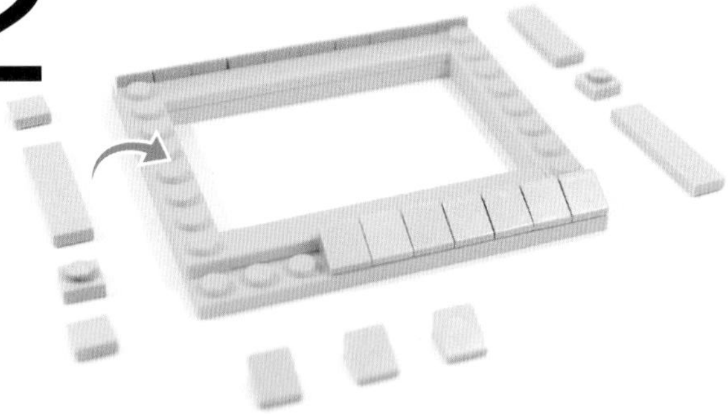

63

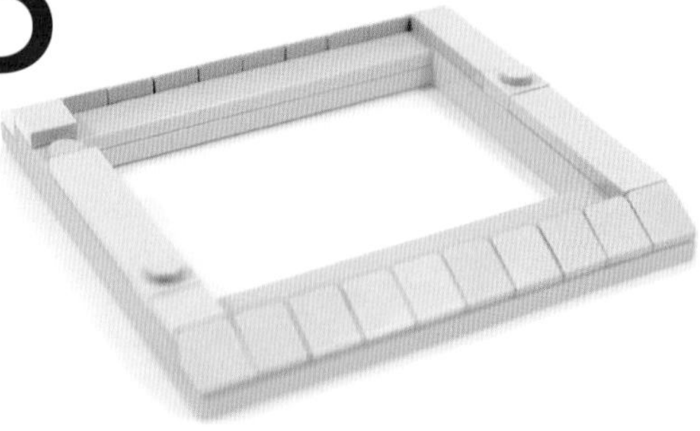

64

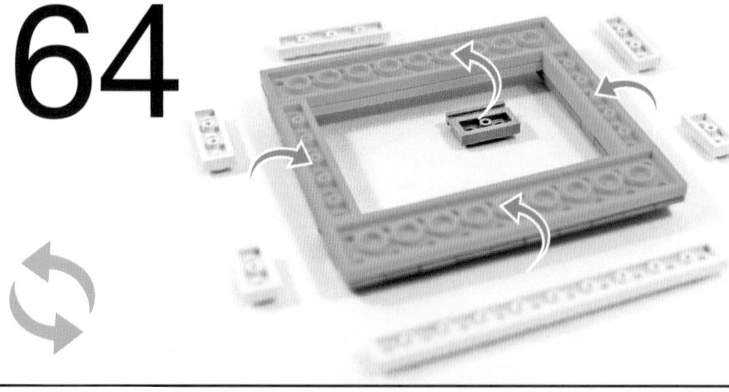

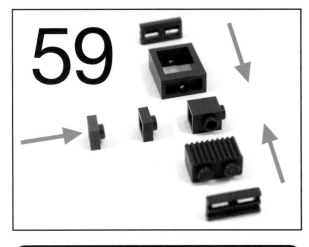

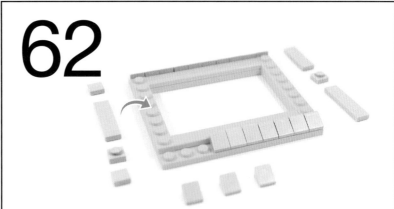

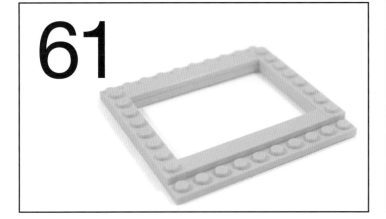

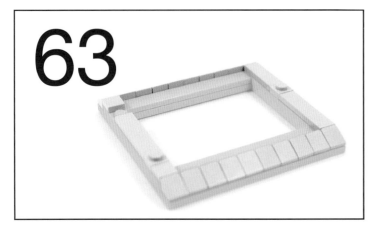

65

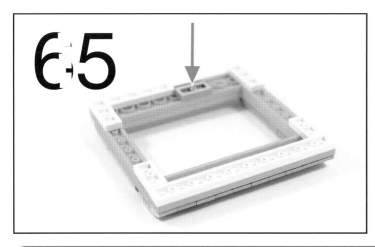

66

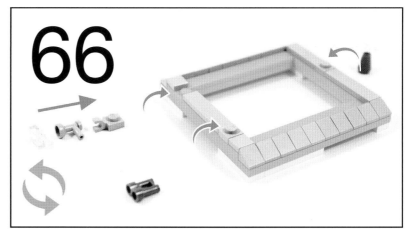

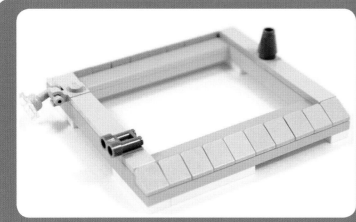

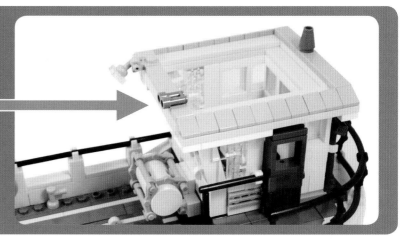

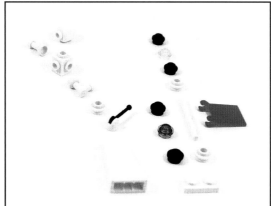

67

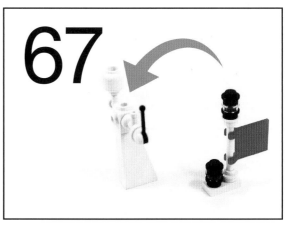

68

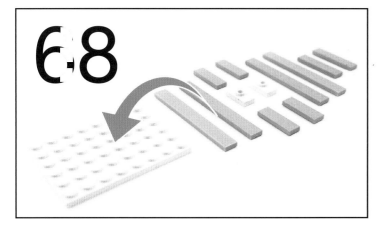

69

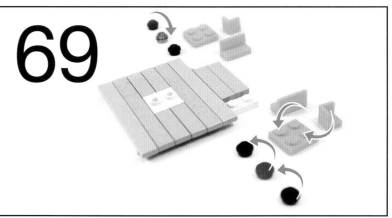

70

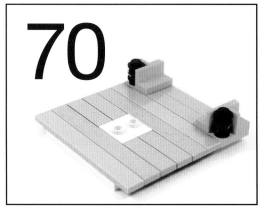
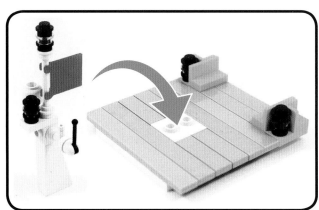
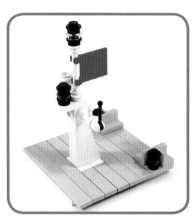

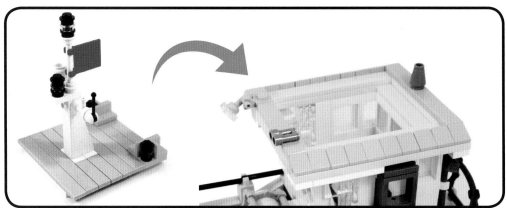
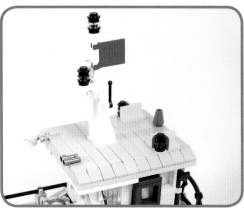

71

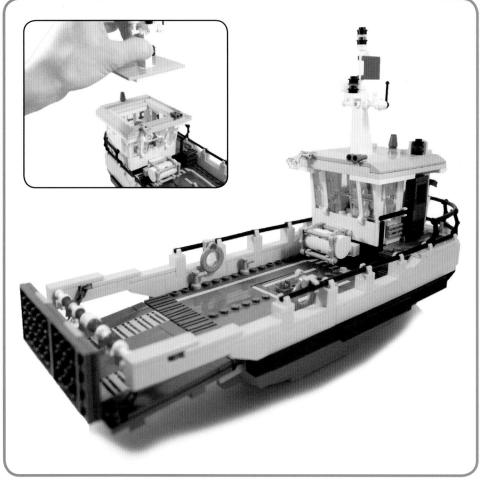

MY FERRY HAS A LOT OF COOL FUNCTIONS AND MOVING PARTS, LIKE THIS RAMP THAT LETS CARS DRIVE RIGHT ON BOARD.

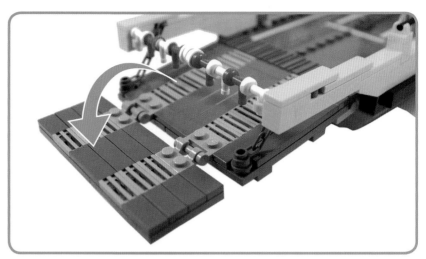
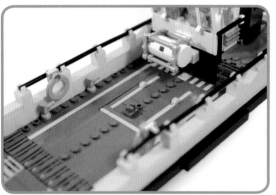
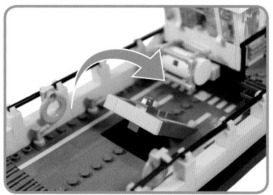
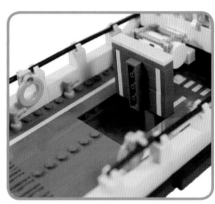
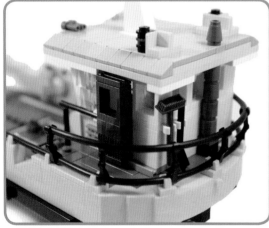
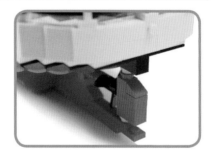
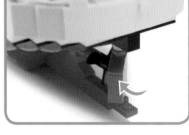

GREAT! WE DID IT! THANK YOU FOR HELPING ME REBUILD MY FERRY, MEGS!

NO PROBLEM. HAPPY TO HELP, ARJAN. THIS IS A VERY NICE FERRY INDEED.

THANKS, MEGS. NORMALLY I DON'T BUILD LEGO MODELS THIS SMALL. YOU SHOULD SEE SOME OF MY OTHER SHIPS; PERHAPS THEY COULD BE INSPIRING FOR YOU, TOO.

COOL, I'D LIKE TO SEE THEM...

Steam Tug: Maarten

Harbor Tug: Smit Bison

VLI-8 Beam Trawler

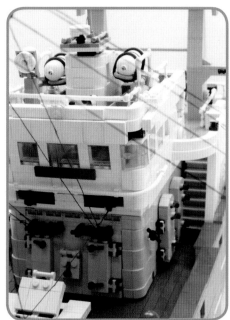

Jacques Cousteau's Calypso

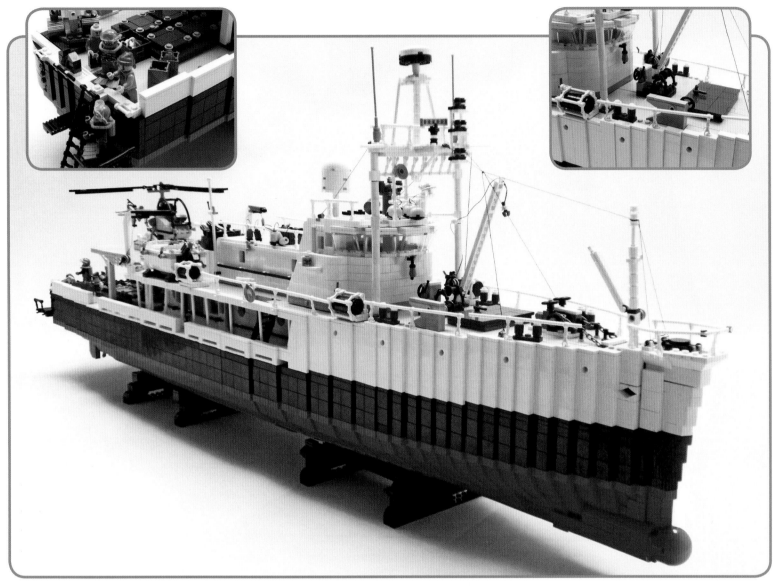

WOW, ARJAN, THOSE ARE SOME EPIC SHIPS!

THANK YOU, MEGS. THEY WERE VERY FUN TO BUILD.

HONK! HONK!

WELL, I'M NOW UP AND RUNNING AGAIN, AND I SEE MY FIRST CUSTOMER IS VERY EAGER TO BOARD!

YEAH, I THINK I'D BETTER GET OUT OF HIS WAY! TAKE GOOD CARE OF MY FRIEND'S CAR.

YOU DON'T HAVE TO WORRY ABOUT THAT, MEGS. IT WILL ARRIVE SAFE AND SOUND.

Megs, come in, Megs!

Fortuitously, my sensors have picked up the Destructor on an uncharted isle. If you hurry, perhaps you can catch up to him.

OK, BRICKBOT! PUNCH IN THE COORDINATES.

GOTTA RUN, ARJAN. THANKS FOR SHARING YOUR SHIPS WITH ME!

GOED ZO, VERY GOOD, MEGS! SEE YOU LATER, TOT ZIENS!

YES, DEFINITELY. TOT ZIENS, ARJAN!

THIS MUST BE THE THE ISLAND. LOOKS LIKE A HURRICANE HAS BLOWN THROUGH HERE! WELL, HELLO DOWN THERE!
megs
AHOY! THAT PINK-HAIRED, LILY-LIVERED SCALLYWAG BLEW MY LOOKOUT HUT TO SMITHEREENS! YOU LOOK LIKE A HANDY BUILDER. WANT TO HELP ME FIX IT?
AHOY, YOURSELF! THE NAME BE MEGS, AND I'D BE HAPPY TO OBLIGE, SIR!

Castaway's Cove

Barney Main

Nickname: SlyOwl

Profession: Engineering Design Student

Nationality: British

Website: *www.flickr.com/photos/27444109@N04/*

Lookout Hut

AS YE CAN SEE IN THE BUILDING PLANS, EACH SIDE OF ME LOOKOUT HUT IS DIFFERENT. KEEP A KEEN EYE ON THE STEPS, ME HEARTIES!

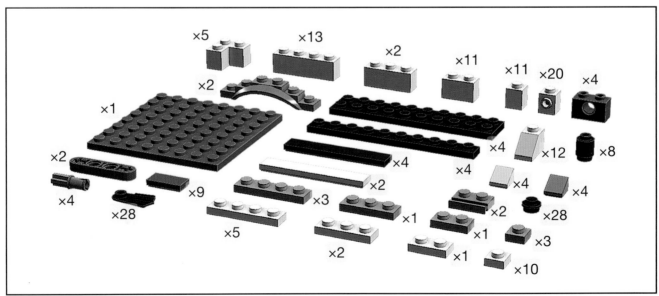

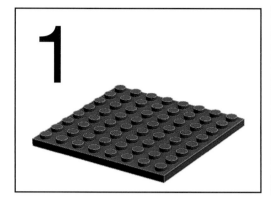

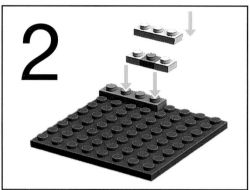

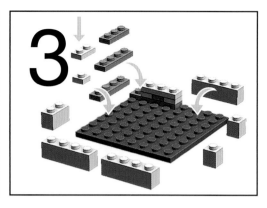

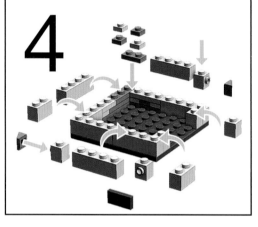

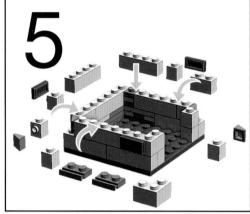

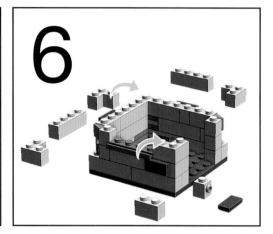

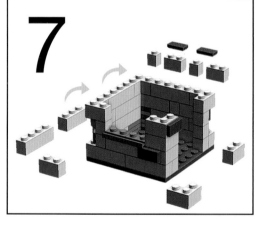

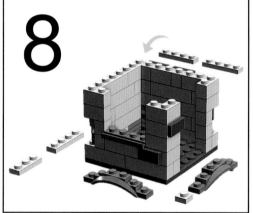

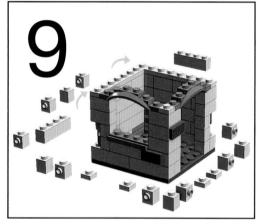

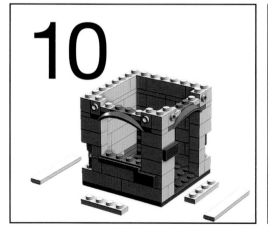

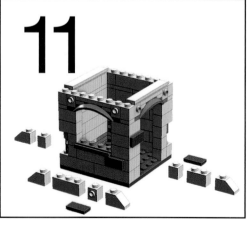

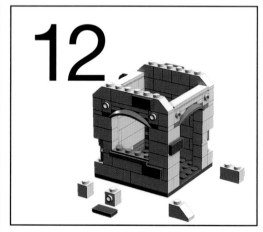

13

14

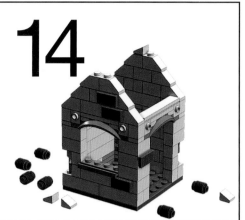

15

16

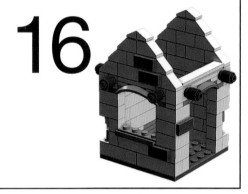

×2

17

18

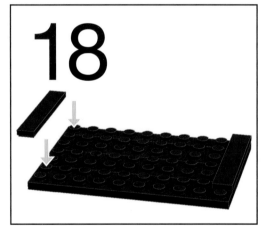

19

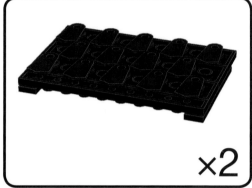

×14

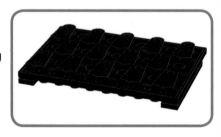

20

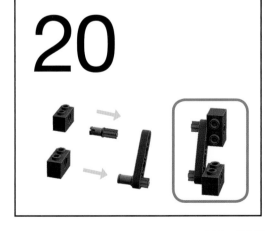

21

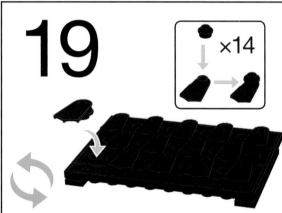

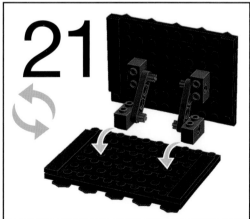

22

A BUILDING LIKE THIS CAN BE ANY SIZE. SCALE YOUR BUILDING TO FIT YOUR ENVIRONMENT. MY ISLAND'S SMALL, SO I KEPT MY HUT SMALL, TOO. JUST BE SURE A MINIFIGURE CAN GET THROUGH THE DOORWAY. HERE ARE SOME DETAILS YOU CAN ADD TO YOUR HUT. YOU'LL NEED PROVISIONS IF YOU'VE BEEN MAROONED!

Building Tip
Try looking at every LEGO element in a creative way. You may discover an amazing new use for it. For example, you can use a flipper as a roof tile, as Barney has done here.

COOL LOOKOUT HUT! WHAT ELSE HAVE YOU BUILT?

HOW ABOUT SOMETHING FOR A LANDLUBBER? A PALM TREE FROM ME ISLAND.

Palm Tree

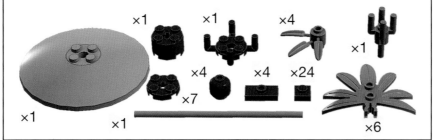

×1 ×1 ×4 ×1
×1 ×4 ×4 ×24
×7
×1 ×1 ×6

Building Tip
Adding flexible tubing in the middle of the trunk allows this palm tree to bend into all sorts of natural shapes.

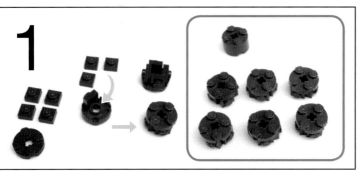

1

2

3

4

WELL, THAR'S SOME NICE LEGO MODELS. DO YE MIND SHOWIN' ME MORE FROM YOUR ISLAND, SIR?

AYE AYE, MEGS, T'WOULD BE ME PLEASURE.

Dock Crane

THIS CRANE BE A LITTLE COMPLICATED TO BUILD, MATEY. PAY CLOSE ATTENTION.

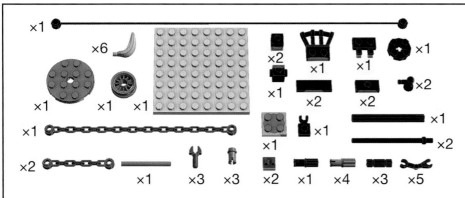

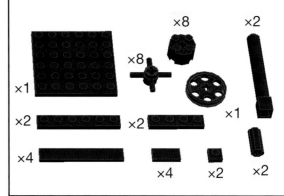

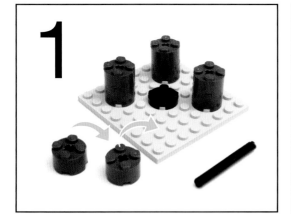

1

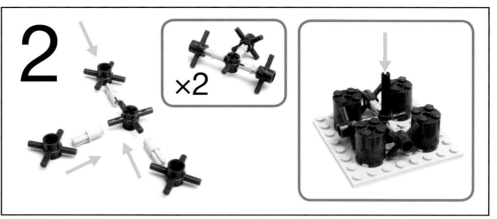

2

×2

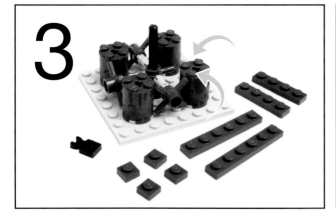

3

4

5

6

7

8

9

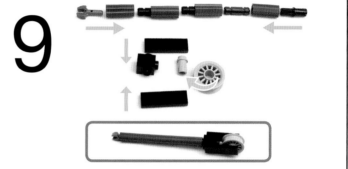

10

11

Raiders Reef

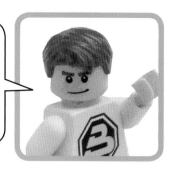

ME BEAUTIFUL ISLAND HAS EVERYTHING A PIRATE NEEDS: A LOVELY BEACH WITH A SHIPWRECK OFF THE PORT SIDE, A DOCK AND CRANE TO UNLOAD SUPPLIES, AND CANNONS TO FEND OFF WOULD-BE INTRUDERS. *ARRR!*

BUILDING JOURNAL

Barney has a lot of cool details in his models, all well suited to a tropical island. His use of slopes to build up a rock face is a great way to landscape. Combining part of an old ship to make a deck and stairway gives it the ramshackle look of flotsom and jetsam. If I build a pirate island, I'll make sure it is made of objects that have washed ashore!

Cannon

 1

 2

 3

Pirate Inspiration

Row Boat

Galleons

BUILDING JOURNAL

Barney's ships are amazing! He adds accent colors, like white and black, to break up the brown of the ship and add interest to what could otherwise be a plain area. The string rigging helps to hold the masts and spars up, and it makes the ship look much more realistic. The string is not official LEGO string, and Barney also made his own sails out of cloth. Maybe I'll try that!

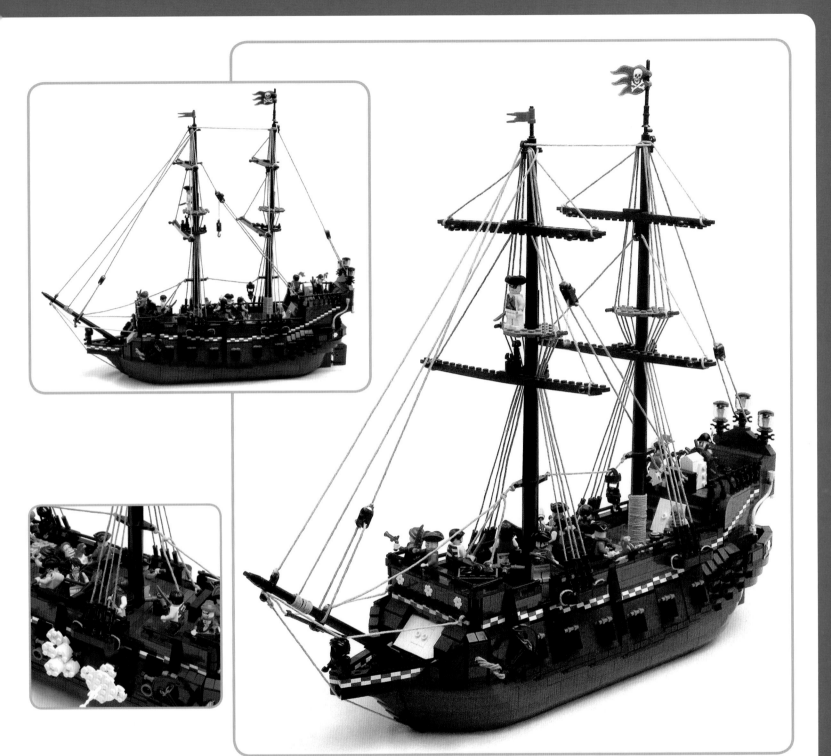

Megs, I have intercepted a transmission about a "royal mess." I think you can be of assistance. Beaming you there now!

I'M ON IT, BRICKBOT. GOTTA GO, BARNEY. CHEERS FOR THE TOUR!

megs

FAIR WINDS, ME BEAUTY!

The Tudors

Birgitte Jonsgard

Nickname: birgburg

Profession: Science Teacher

Nationality: Norwegian

Website: *www.flickr.com/people/birgburg/*

Gingerbread House

THIS IS A TUDOR-STYLE HOUSE, WHICH MEANS YOU CAN SEE THE STRUCTURAL POSTS AND BEAMS. BE SURE TO TAKE YOUR TIME BUILDING THE ROOF AND KEEP AN EYE OUT FOR HIDDEN FEATURES.

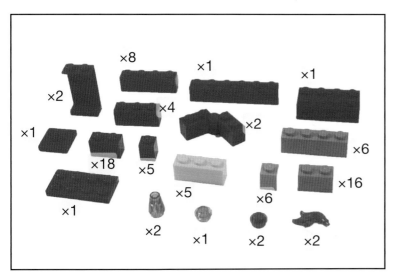

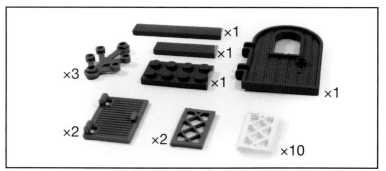

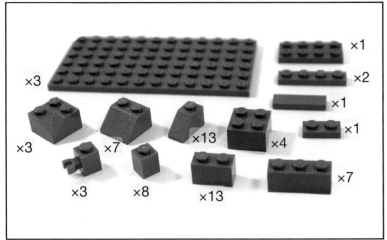

×3 ×3 ×7 ×13 ×4 ×1 ×2 ×1 ×1 ×3 ×8 ×13 ×7

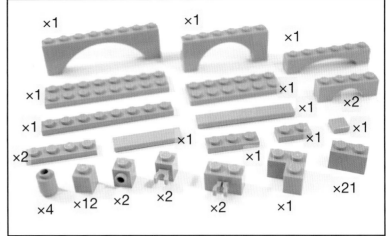

×1 ×1 ×1 ×1 ×1 ×2 ×1 ×1 ×1 ×2 ×1 ×2 ×4 ×12 ×2 ×2 ×2 ×1 ×21

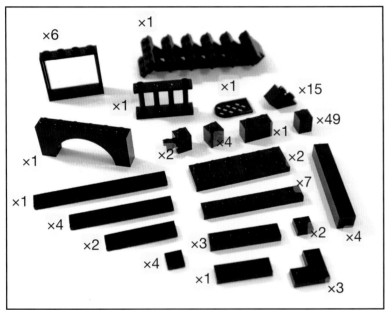

×6 ×1 ×1 ×1 ×15 ×1 ×49 ×2 ×4 ×1 ×1 ×2 ×1 ×7 ×4 ×2 ×2 ×3 ×4 ×1 ×3 ×4

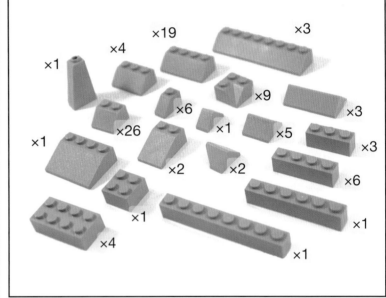

×1 ×4 ×19 ×3 ×9 ×6 ×3 ×1 ×26 ×1 ×5 ×3 ×2 ×2 ×6 ×1 ×4 ×1 ×1

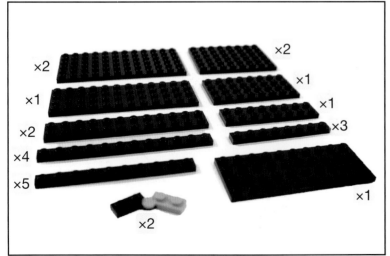

×2 ×2 ×1 ×1 ×1 ×1 ×2 ×3 ×4 ×5 ×1 ×2

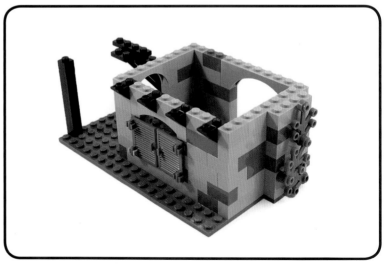

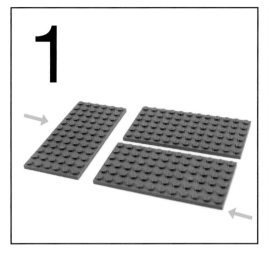

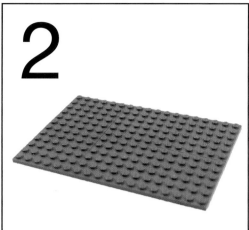

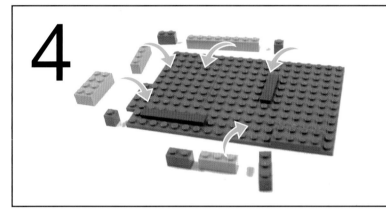

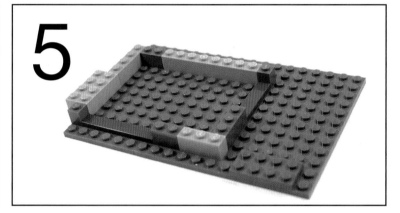

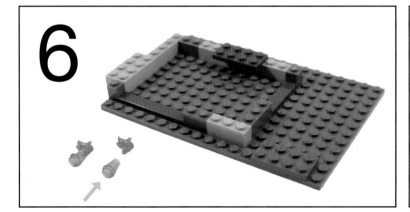

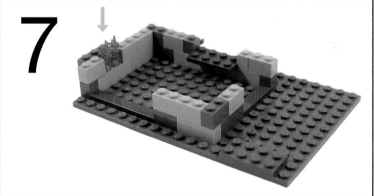

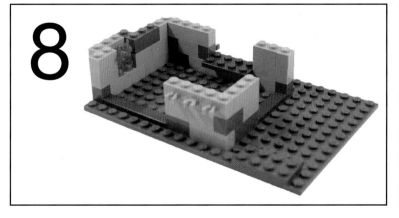

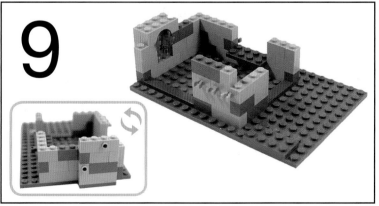

10

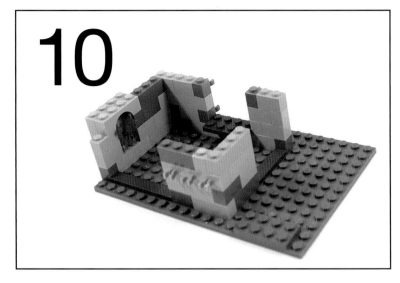

11

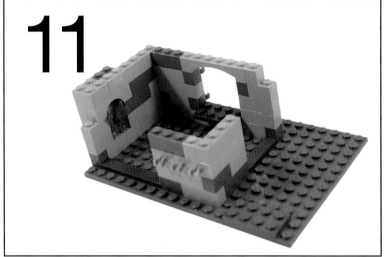

12

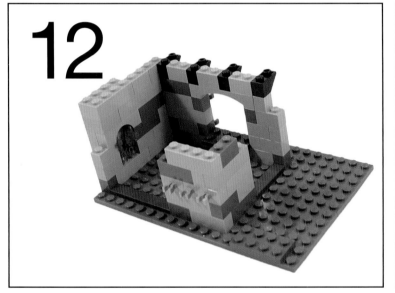

13

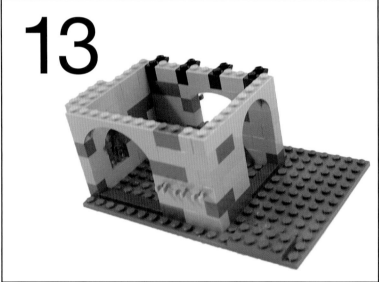

14

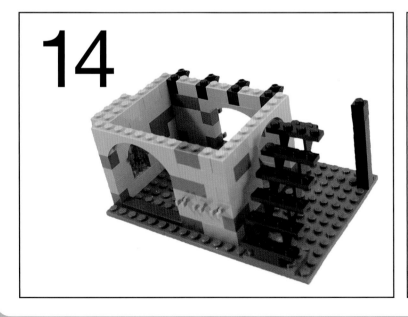

15

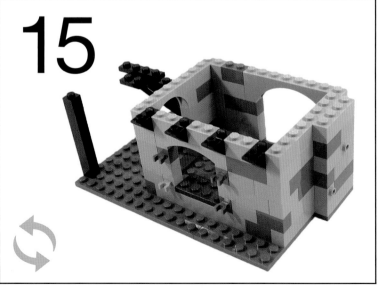

16

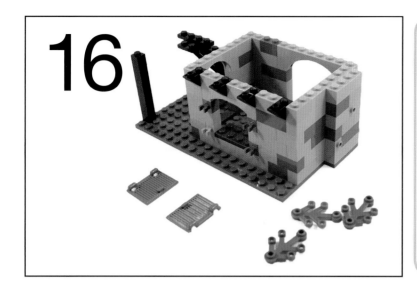

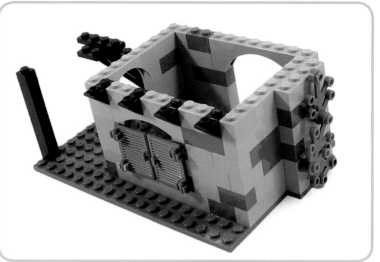

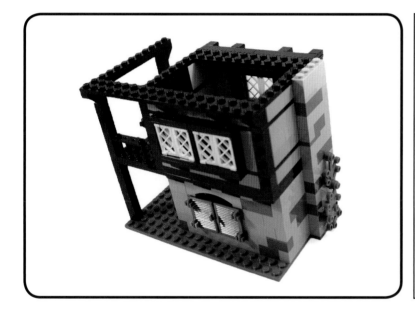

17

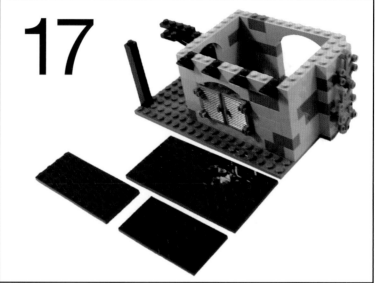

18

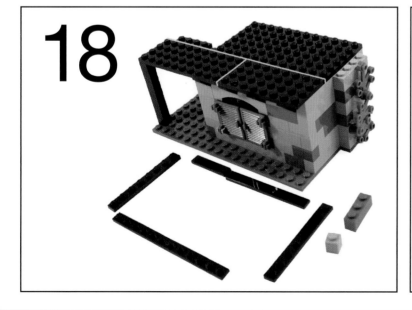

19

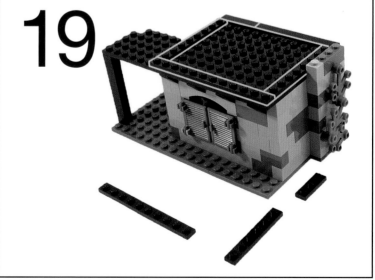

20

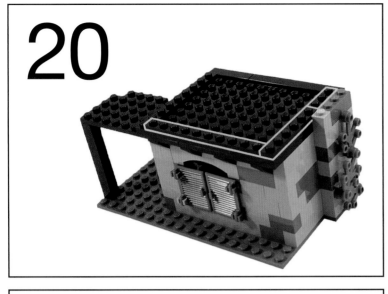

21

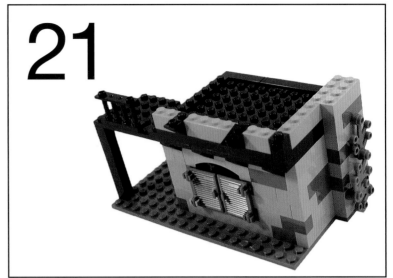

22

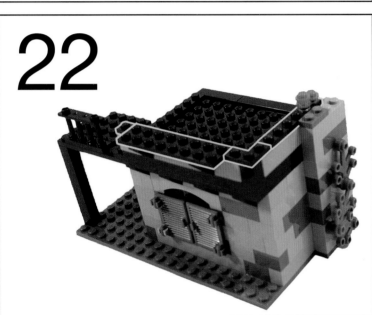

23

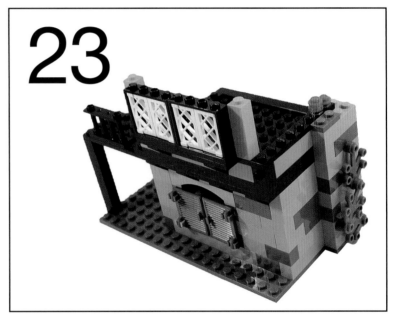

24

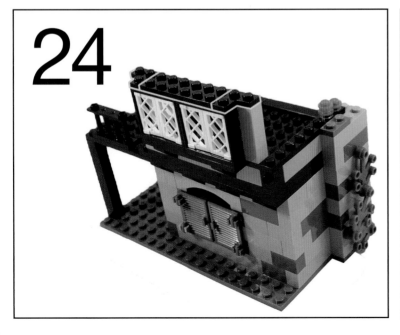

25

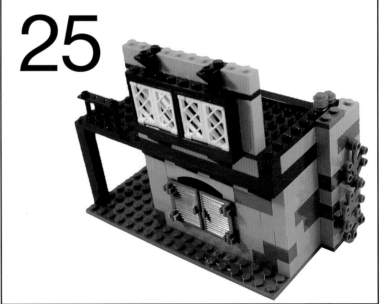

26

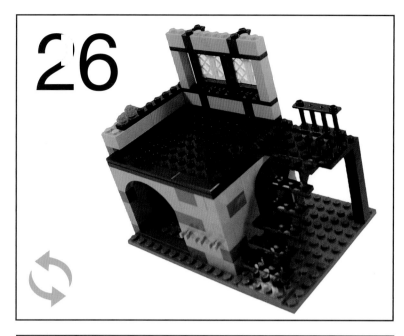

27

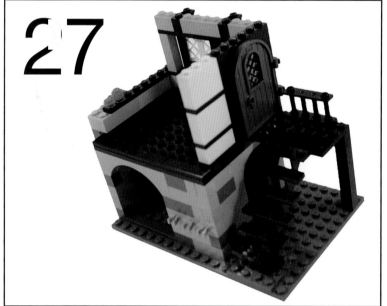

28

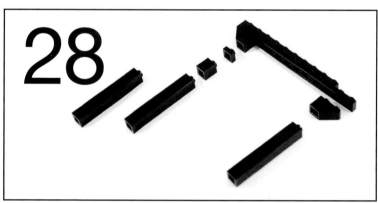

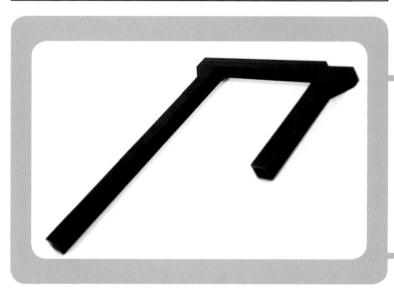

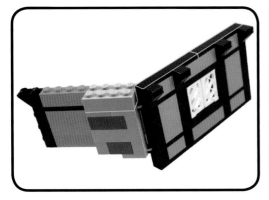

29

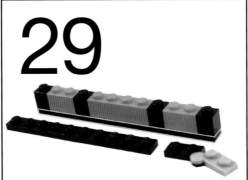

30

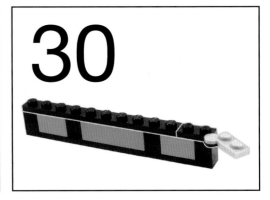

31

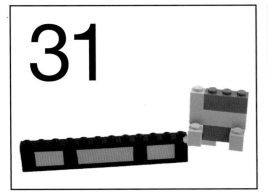

32

33

34

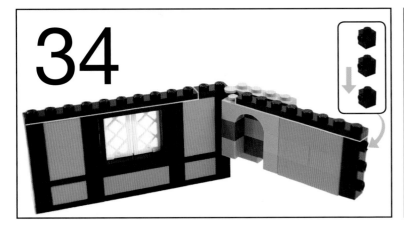

35

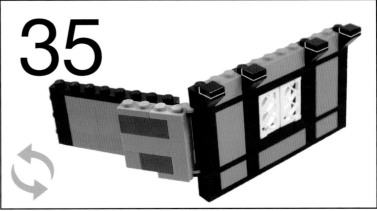

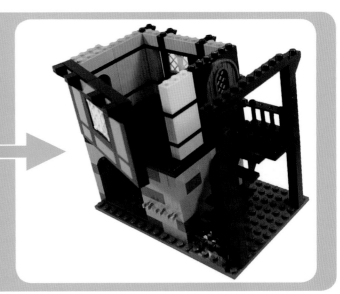

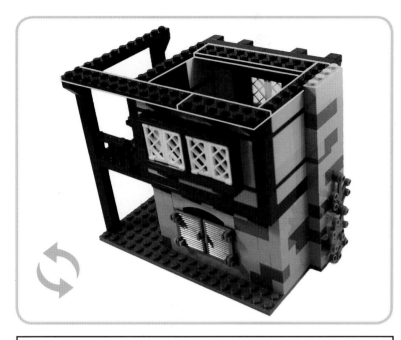

36

37

38

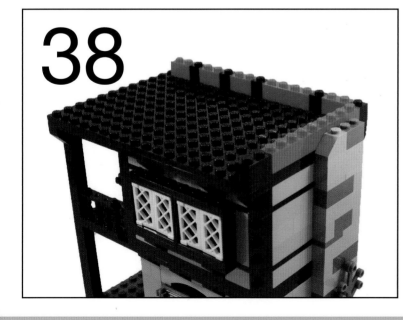

39

40

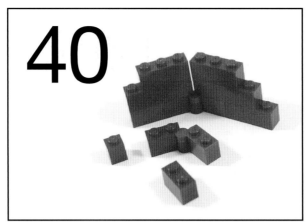

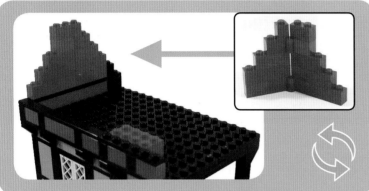

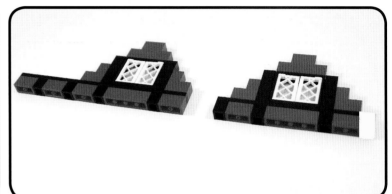

41

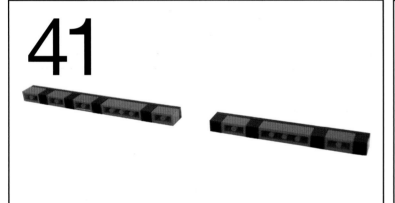

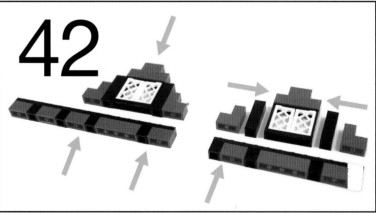

42

Building Tip
Using black or brown bricks, you can create a gridded frame. Then you can fill the spaces with brighter colors—in this case, yellow, orange, and red. This produces a nice Tudor look.

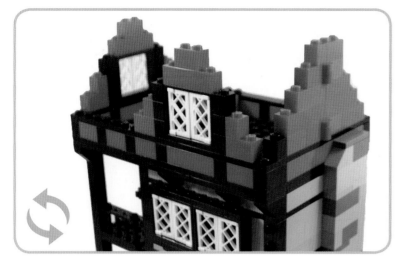

43

44

45

46

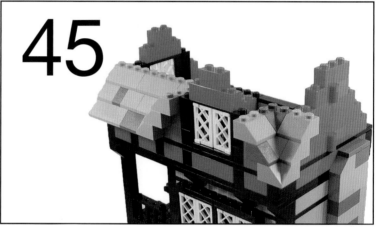
47

48

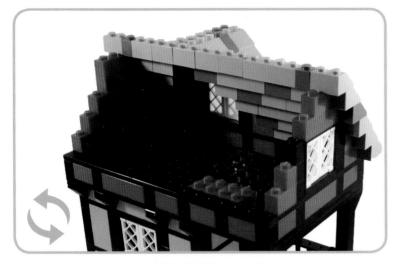

49

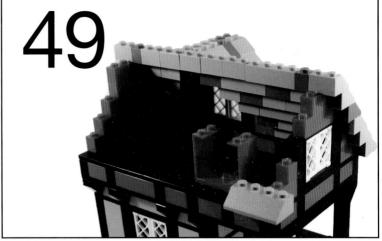

50

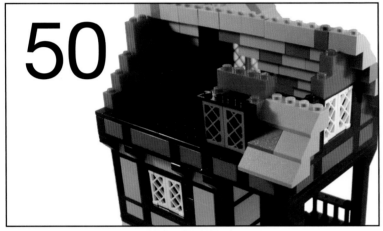

51

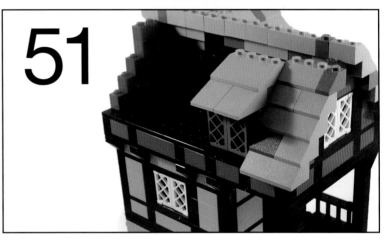

52

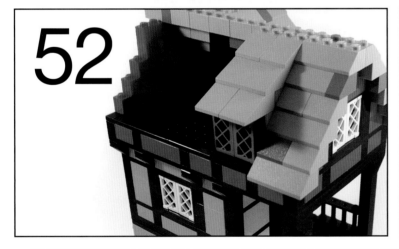

53

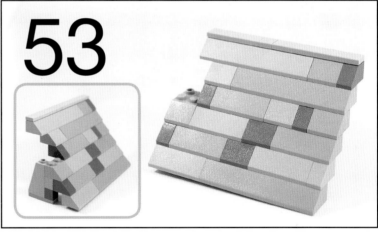

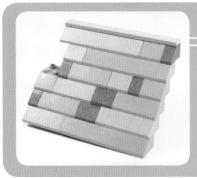

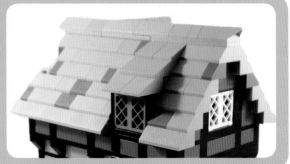

54

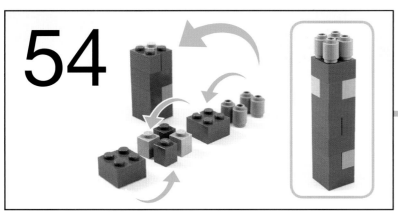 

55

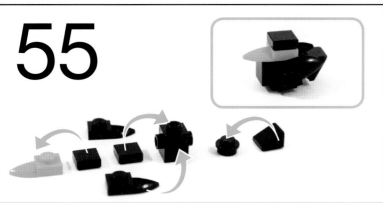 

Building Tip
Before you start building, it might help to sketch your ideas on paper to work out space and perspective.

MY HOUSE FEATURES SIDES THAT OPEN. THIS BUILDING DOESN'T HAVE TO BE A HOUSE. BY CHANGING THE INTERIOR, YOU CAN MAKE IT ANYTHING YOU WISH: A BAKERY, A BUTCHER'S SHOP, A SMITHY, OR A TAVERN.

Building Tip
When building a house, it is nice to include a wall or two that can open, so you can easily place furniture and minifigures inside.

ONCE YOU HAVE BUILT YOUR HOUSE, ADD SOME FURNITURE TO COMPLETE IT.

Four-Poster Bed

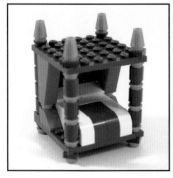

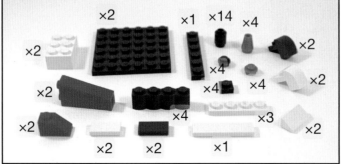

×2 ×1 ×14 ×4
×2
×2 ×2
×2
×4
×4 ×4 ×2
×4
×2 ×3
×2 ×2 ×1 ×2

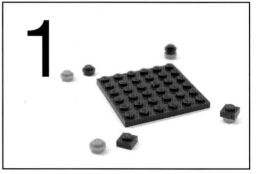

1

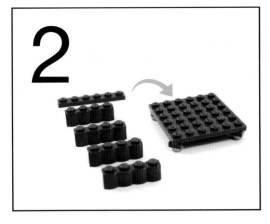

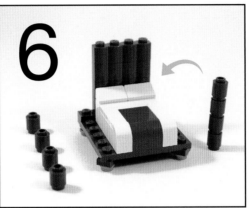

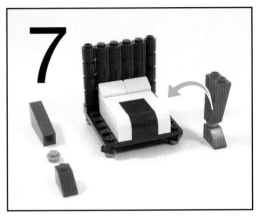

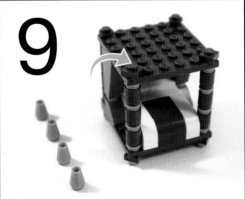

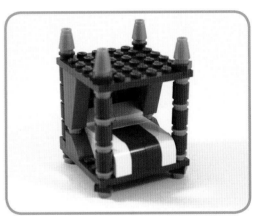

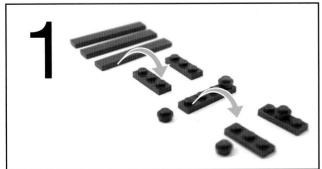

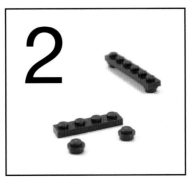

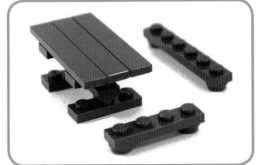

Dining Table

Quilt Bed

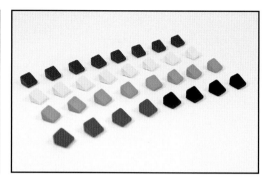

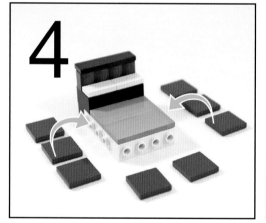
1

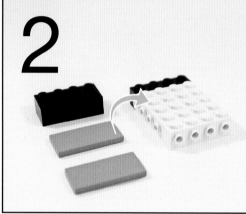
2

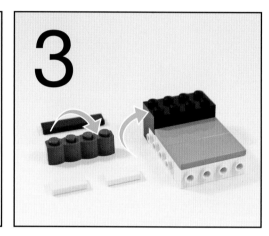
3

4

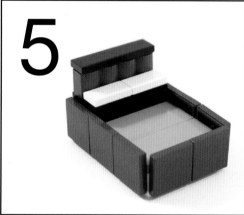
5

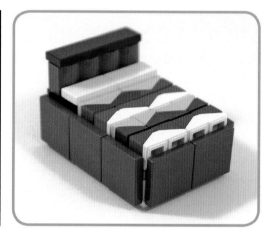

I'VE AN IDEA! LET'S ADD A GARDEN AND MAKE THINGS NICE FOR THE NEW FAMILY.

GOOD THINKING! WHY DON'T WE START WITH SOME OF YOUR PLANTS AND TREES?

In the Garden

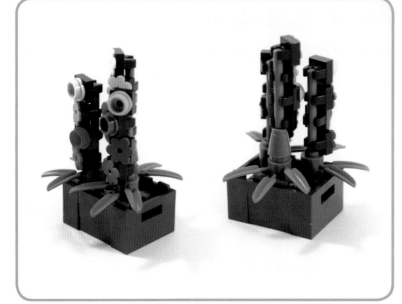

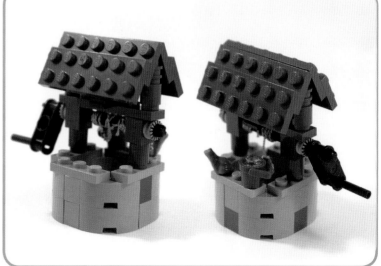

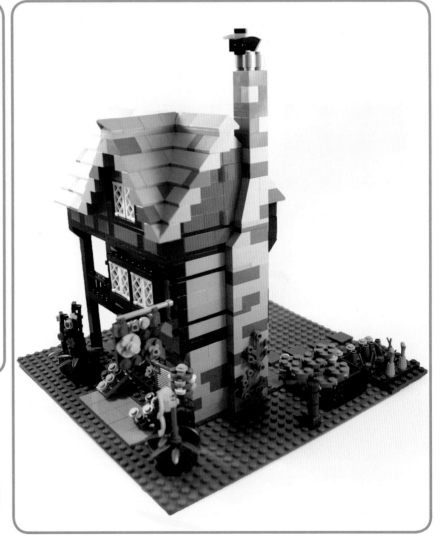

THERE, THAT LOOKS MUCH BETTER! JUST IN TIME. YOU GO HIDE, MEGS, AND I'LL CHANGE INTO PERIOD DRESS SO THE NEW FAMILY DOESN'T GET CONFUSED.

Building Tip
Flowers and plants really brings a LEGO display to life. It only takes a few brightly colored LEGO bricks to build some plants, and an old barrel or crate can make a nice planter box for them.

Snugburg

WELCOME TO SNUGBURG! THERE IS A LOT GOING ON HERE. EACH SIDE OF TOWN TELLS A DIFFERENT STORY.

Building Tip

When building a town or other large LEGO structure, the best way to keep a coherent look is to repeat design features in several places. This will prevent things from becoming too chaotic and give your model a cleaner look.

Life in Snugburg

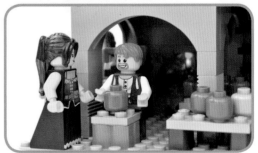

BUILDING JOURNAL

I really enjoyed meeting Birgitte and seeing her brilliant models! Her use of bright colors with more muted black and brown timber framing creates a medieval look that's fun and whimsical. She told me how she likes to build scenes and create stories for her minifigures. This brings them to life. Snugburg is cleverly built on a single 48×48 stud LEGO base plate and is a great example of how you can build an entire city incorporating different looks into each side within a condensed space. The stonework of the castle blends seamlessly into the Tudor buildings. I should keep these techniques in mind for the next addition to my Idea Lab!

Building Tip
You can group colors—for example, warm colors like yellow, orange, red, and brown or cold colors like blues and purples. Or you can contrast them, as Birgitte has, to make parts of your model stand out.

WOW, SNUGBURG LOOKS LIKE A REALLY FUN PLACE TO LIVE! BUT I HAVE TO GET BACK ON THE TRAIL OF THE DESTRUCTOR NOW. THANKS FOR SHOWING ME AROUND, BIRGITTE!

YOU ARE MOST WELCOME, MEGS. IT WAS MY PLEASURE. GOOD LUCK APPREHENDING THAT MAD DESTRUCTOR!

On Set: STAR CLUTCH

Tommy Williamson

Nickname: Geekytom

Profession: Brick Artist

Nationality: American

Website: *www.bricknerd.com/*

Galactic Adventurer

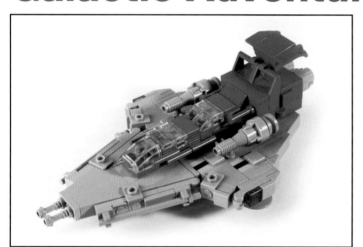

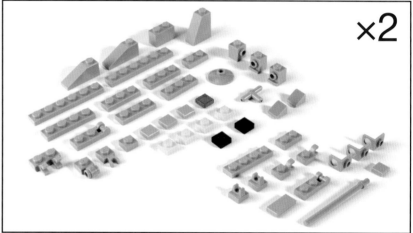

×2

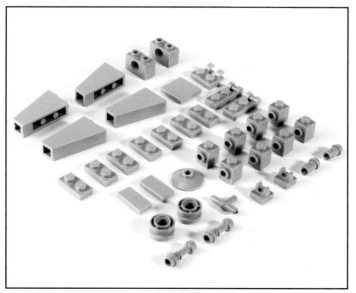

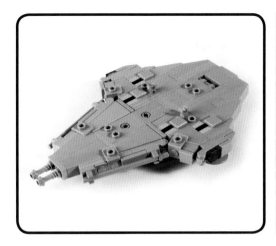

1

2

3

4

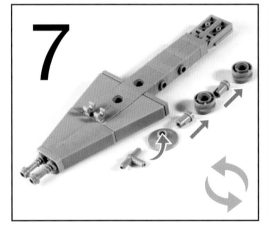

5

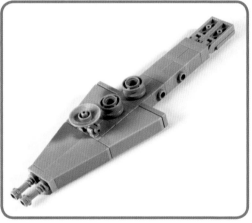

6

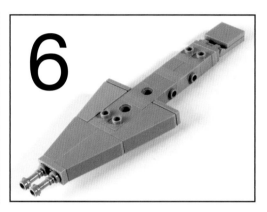

7

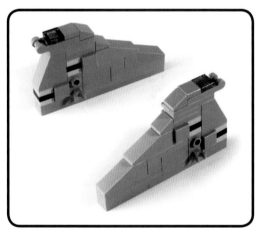

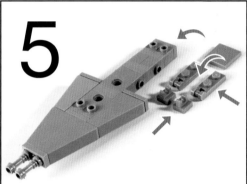

8

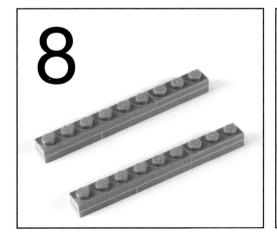

9

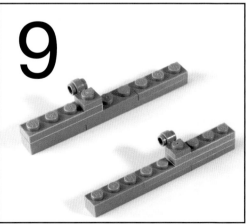

10

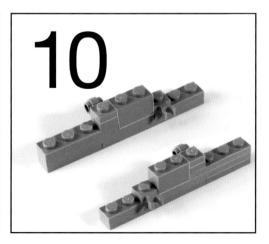

11

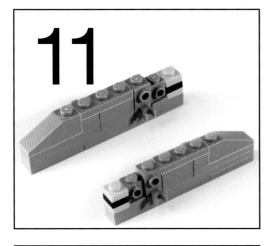

12

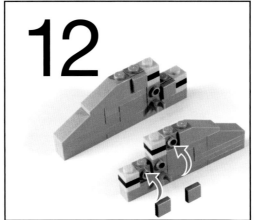

13

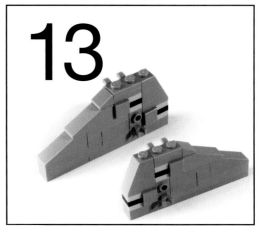

14

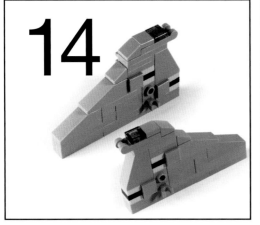

15

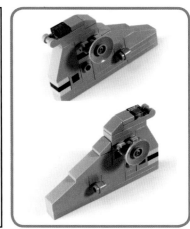

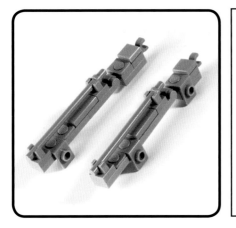

16

17

NOW YOU JUST HAVE TO BUILD THE OTHER SIDE, MIRORRING THE SUBASSEMBLY ABOVE. NOTICE THAT THE LIGHT ON THE WING TIP IS GREEN ON THE OTHER SIDE.

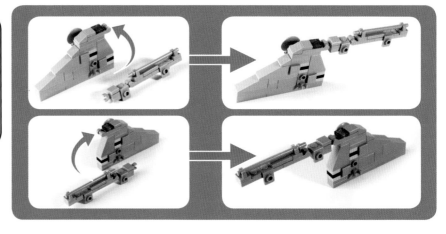

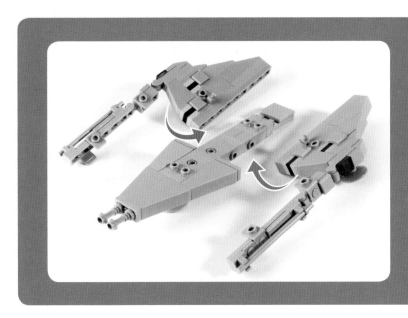

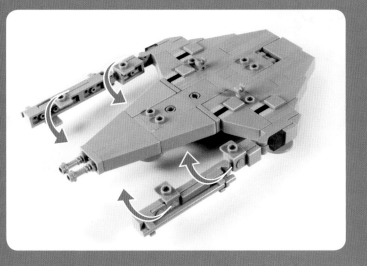

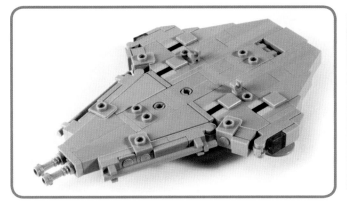

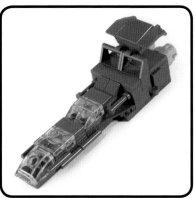

18

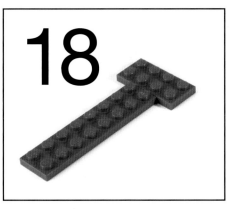

19

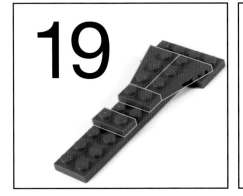

20

21

22

23

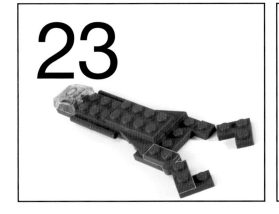

24

25

26

27

28
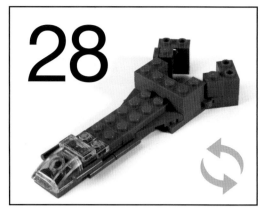

29
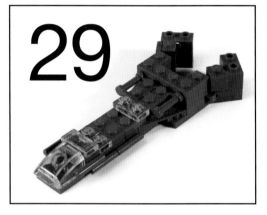

30
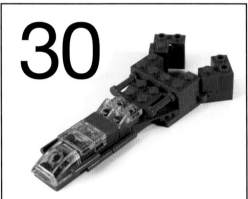

31
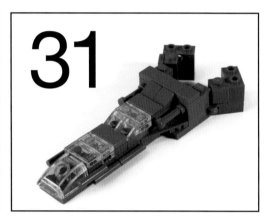

32
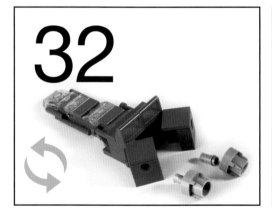

33
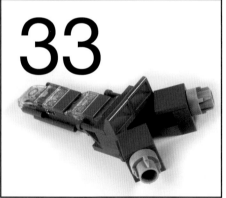

34

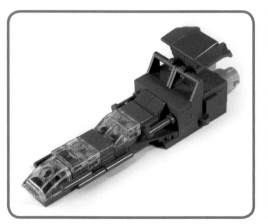

35
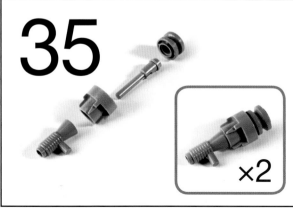

×2

Building Tip
Don't let a missing part stop you from experimenting. You can always switch out the part later, so keep building and try using other parts or colors.

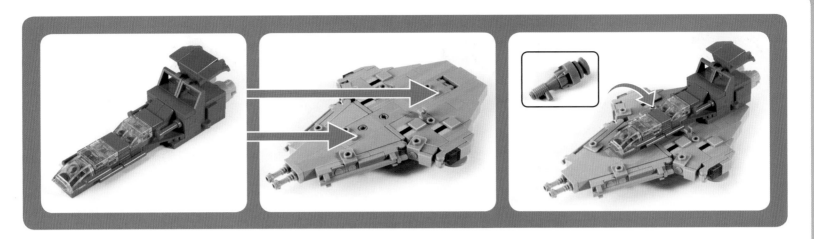

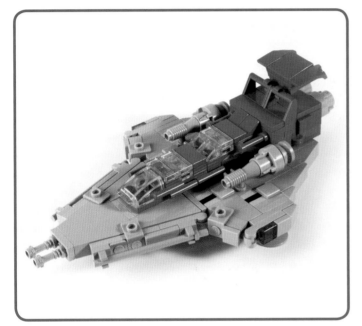

WOW, I THOUGHT YOU SAID THIS WAS A MINIATURE. IT'S HUGE!

YEAH, I GUESS YOU COULD CALL IT A "BIGATURE." IT'S ACTUALLY ONE-QUARTER SCALE. IMAGINE IF THE FULL-SIZED SHIP WERE IN HERE!

IT WOULD BE HARD TO SHOOT. FOR THIS TYPE OF SHOT, WE USE A MOTION CONTROL CAMERA. IT'S LIKE A ROBOT ARM WITH A CAMERA ON THE END. IT ALLOWS FOR PRECISE, REPEATABLE MOVES SO WE CAN ADD SPECIAL EFFECTS.

WELL, LET'S SEE IF THIS DESTRUCTOR GUY LEFT ANY MESSES ON THE OTHER STAGES.

Movie Camera

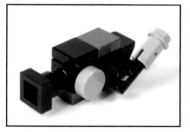

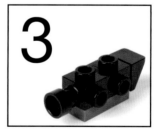

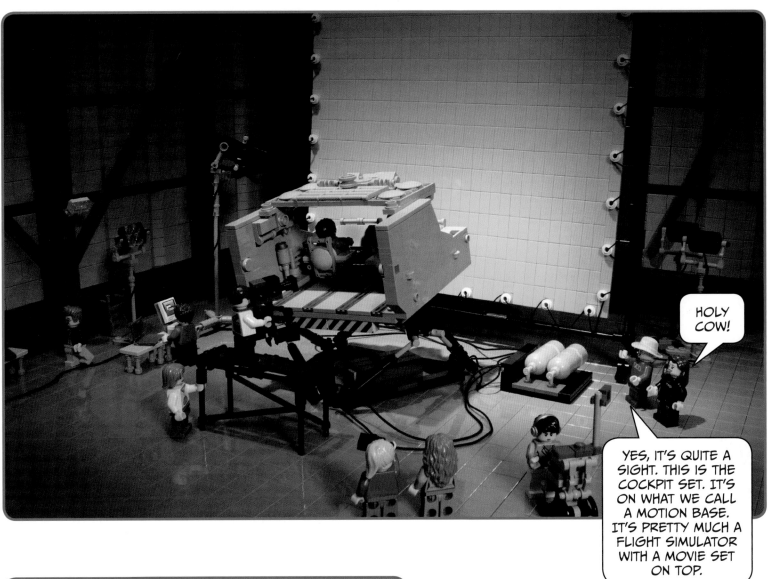

HOLY COW!

YES, IT'S QUITE A SIGHT. THIS IS THE COCKPIT SET. IT'S ON WHAT WE CALL A MOTION BASE. IT'S PRETTY MUCH A FLIGHT SIMULATOR WITH A MOVIE SET ON TOP.

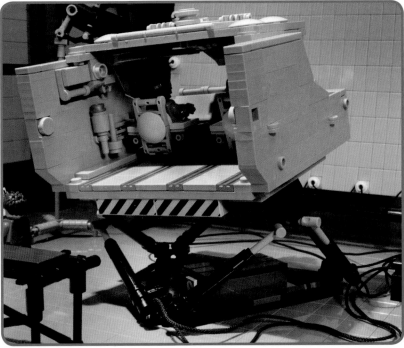

AWESOME. WHAT'S THAT BIG GREEN THING?

THAT'S A GREEN SCREEN. WE USE IT WHEN WE HAVE TO PUT IN A SPECIAL EFFECT LATER. IN THIS CASE, OUTER SPACE WILL BE VISIBLE THROUGH THE SHIP'S WINDOWS.

5K Light

 **1**

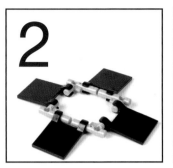 **2**

 **3**

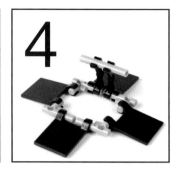 **4**

5

6

7

8

9

10

11

12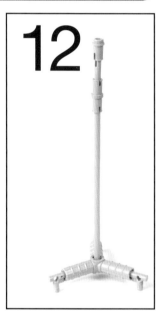

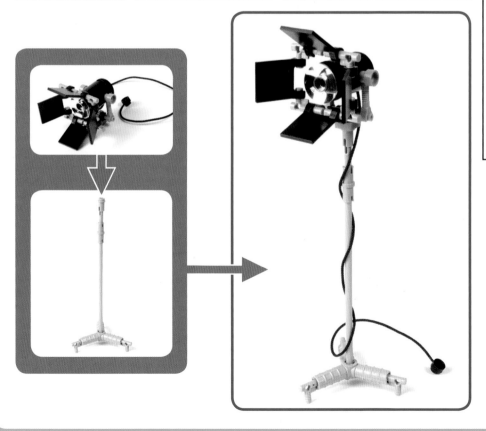

Building Tip
Sometimes playing with and connecting random LEGO pieces (called tablescrapping) can lead to amazing discoveries and inspiration. When you find some spare time and have a load of LEGO bricks in front of you, start sticking them together. Don't overthink it, just build and see what you come up with.

WELCOME TO STAGE 12!

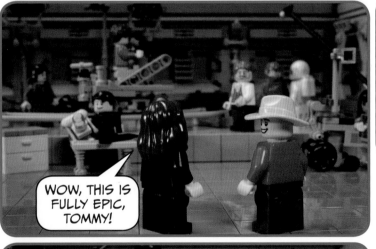

WOW, THIS IS FULLY EPIC, TOMMY!

YEAH, I STILL GET A KICK OUT OF THIS STUFF EVEN AFTER DOING IT FOR AGES. TODAY WE'RE SHOOTING A SCENE IN A CORRIDOR. TOMORROW IT WILL BE AN AIRLOCK. IT'S JUST SO COOL.

HELLO, STEVEN. THIS IS MY FRIEND MEGS. I'M GIVING HER A TOUR. MEGS, THIS IS STEVEN, THE DIRECTOR.

NICE TO MEET YOU, MEGS. ACTUALLY, WE'RE A PERSON DOWN—WOULD YOU BE OPEN TO SHOOTING A LITTLE SCENE?

SURE. I GUESS UNTIL WE TRACE THE DESTRUCTOR I HAVE A LITTLE TIME.

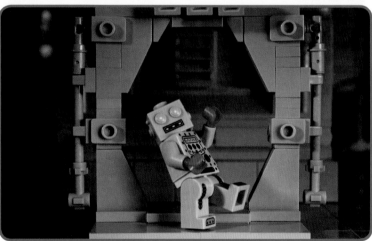

BUILDING JOURNAL

As we wandered through Tommy's epic movie set, I felt like I was on a real Hollywood studio lot! Everything in it is exactly as you'd expect— proper movie cameras, lights, rigging, and green screens! He taught me a lot about the process of filming a movie; I could always use some of these techniques on a smaller scale to create my own studio to shoot some movies.

It was super cool to be filmed as an extra in a movie, too. Will I end up on the cutting-room floor or make it to final cut? Only time will tell!

Destruction Zone

Tyler Clites

Nickname: Legohaulic

Profession: Freelance LEGO Artist

Nationality: American

Website: *www.flickr.com/photos/legohaulic/*

Recycle Wrex

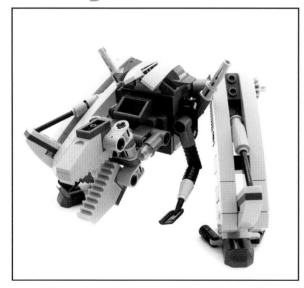

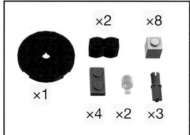

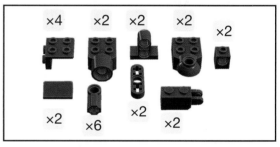

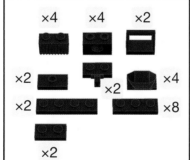

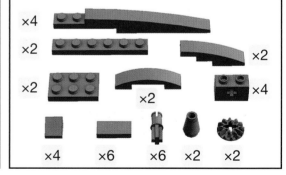

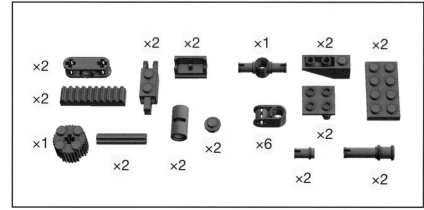

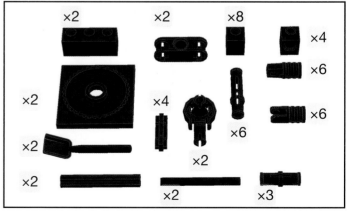

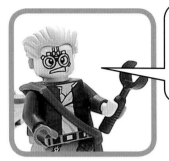

THIS ROBOT HAS SOME TRICKY STEPS, SO STUDY THE BREAKDOWN CLOSELY.

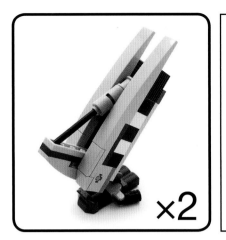

×2

1

2

3

4

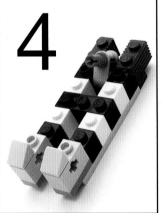

5

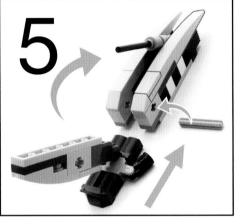

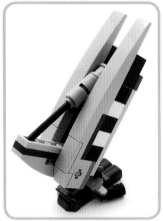

6

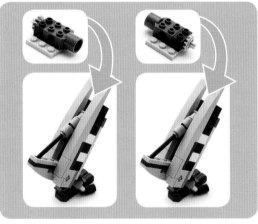

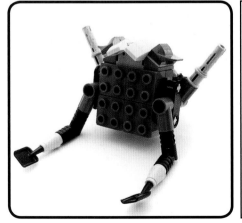

7

8

9

10

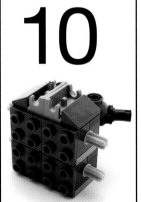

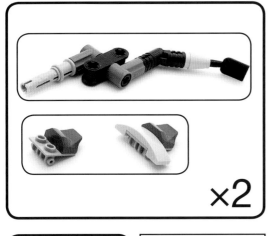

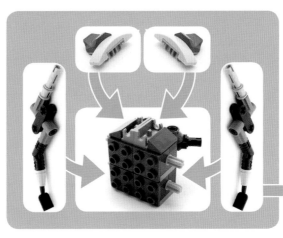

11

12

×2

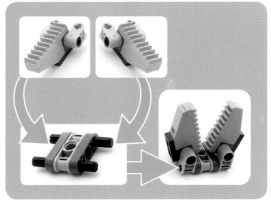

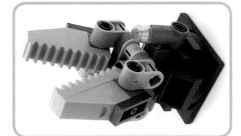

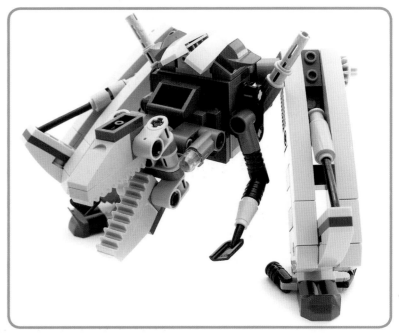

HE IS AWESOME!

YES, HIS POWERFUL JAWS SHOULD MAKE QUICK WORK OF THE RUBBLE. WE MAY EVEN BE ABLE TO CREATE SOMETHING FROM THESE BRICKS TO HELP YOU GET AROUND SAFELY.

THERE ARE SOME NICE BITS AND PIECES AROUND HERE. I'M SURE WE CAN CREATE SOMETHING COOL.

Sludge Puppy

THE MIGHTY SLUDGE PUPPY IS QUITE A TRICKY BUILD. I WOULD RECOMMEND THAT YOU HAVE A GOOD GRASP OF LEGO BUILDING BEFORE TRYING TO TACKLE THIS MODEL! DON'T GO TOO FAST AND KEEP A KEEN EYE ON ALL OF THE SUBASSEMBLIES.

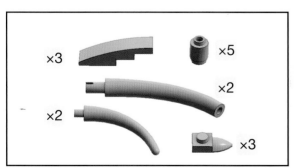

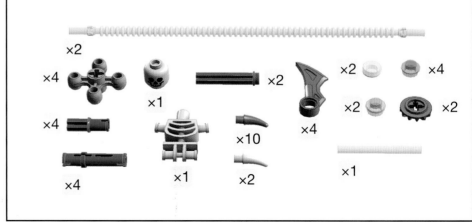

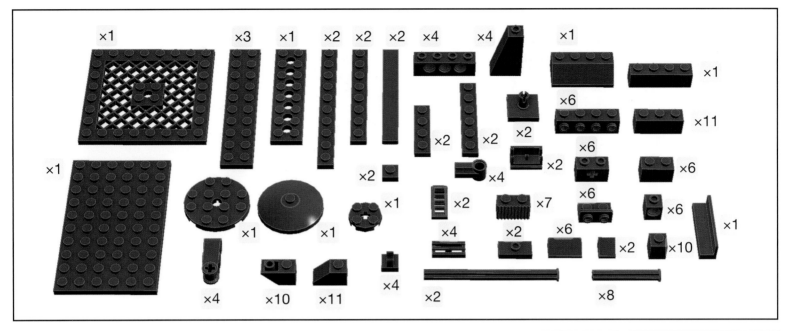

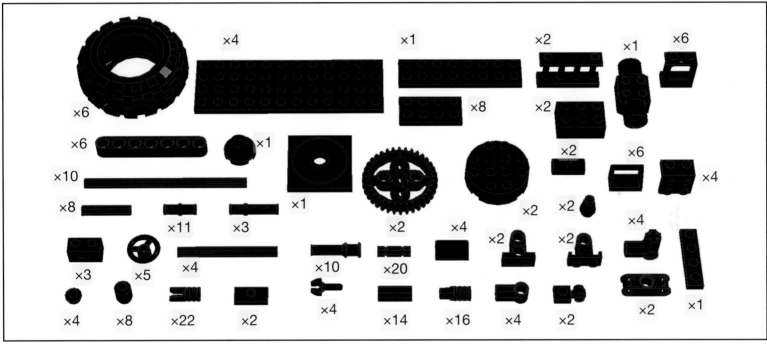

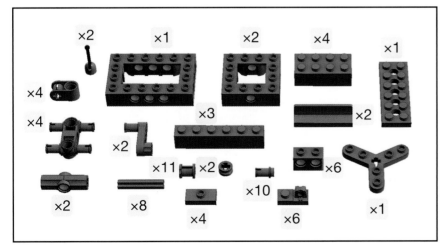

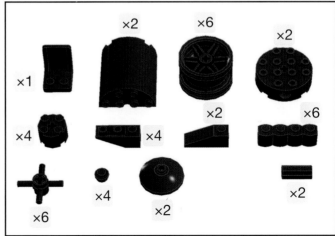

1

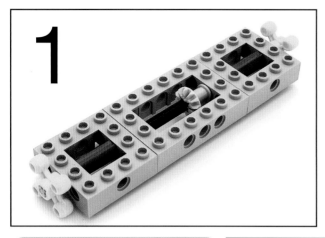

×2

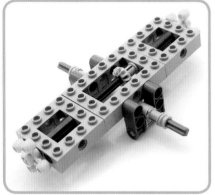

2

3

4

×2

5

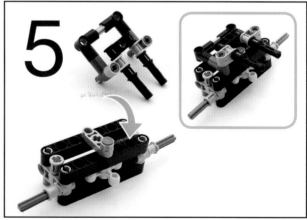

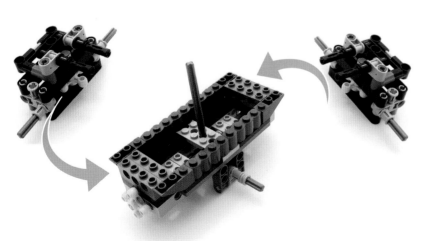

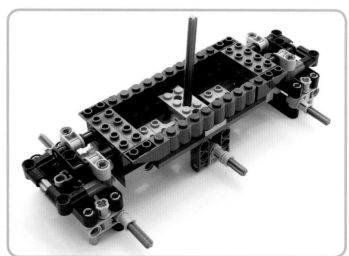

6

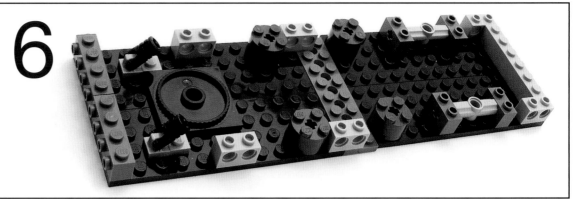

7

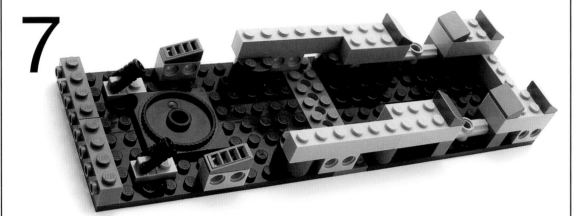

Building Tip
The trick to making your models look like they belong in a post-apocalyptic world is to make them look damaged, repaired, or built out of scavenged parts.

8

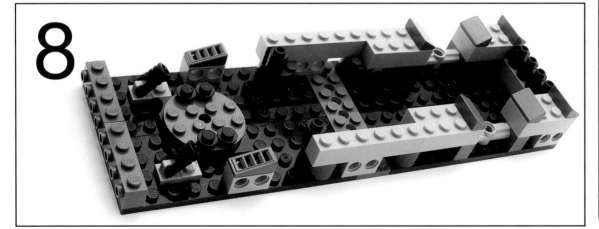

9

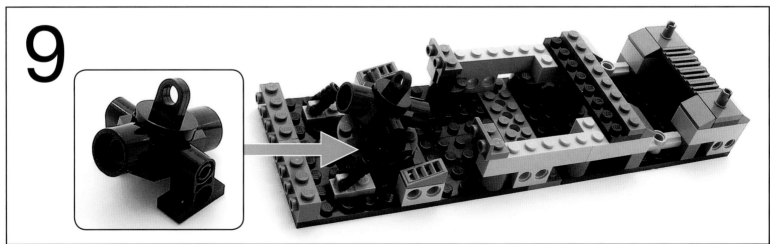

10

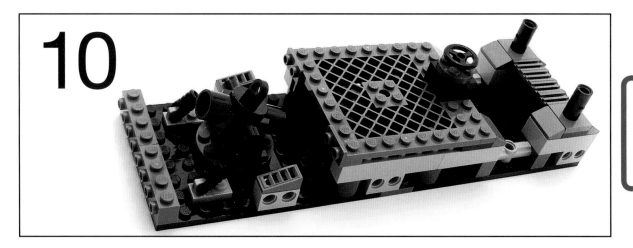

Building Tip
Spikes, blades, darker colors, and skeletons are all items that help give your models a post-disaster look.

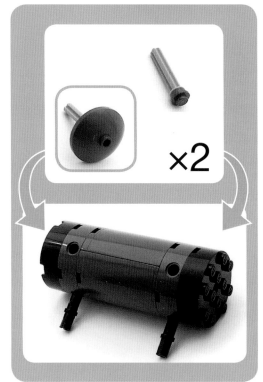

×2

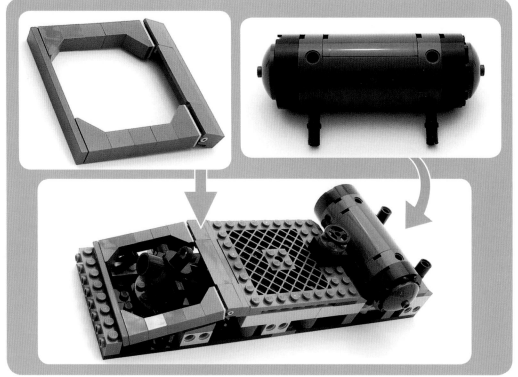

11

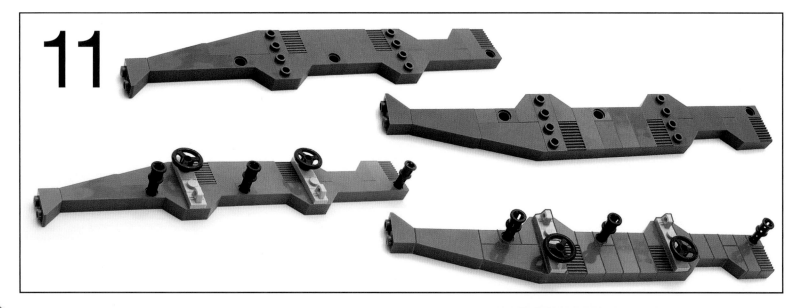

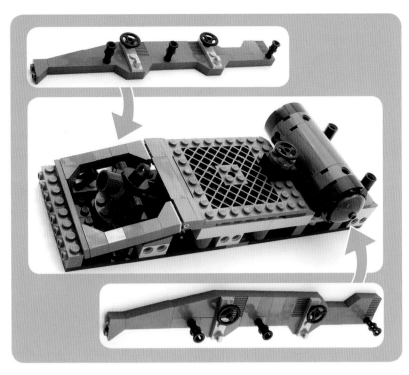

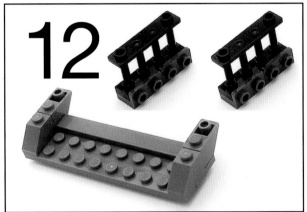

12

13

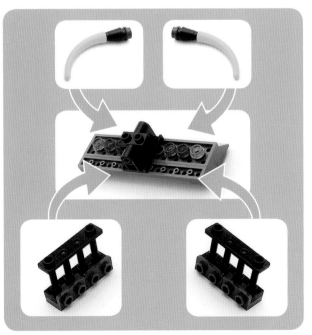

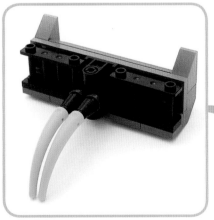

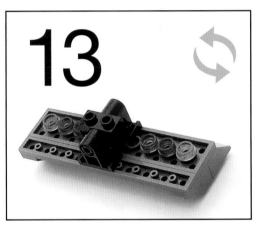

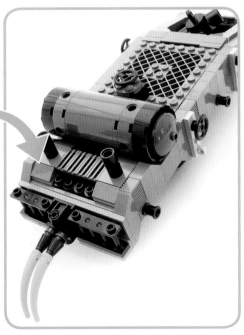

 **14**

 **15**

16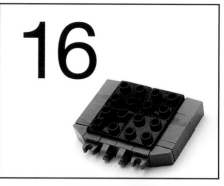

17

18

 ×2

19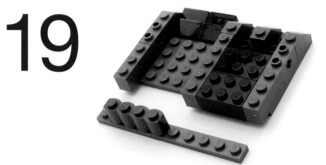

20

21 ×4

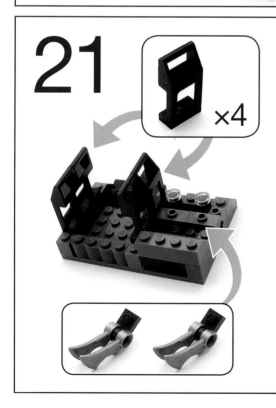

BUILDING JOURNAL

Tyler's models are out of this world. He told me that, for him, the more unusual the idea, the better. His process usually begins with making sketches or finding images that inspire him. Then he starts building—finding the defining features of the model and fitting them all together. For his post-apocalyptic world, muted colors like greys and tans create a dingy, dusty, and broken end-of-civilization atmosphere.

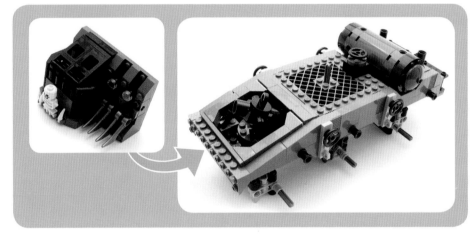

×6

Building Tip
Adding six or more wheels
will instantly turn any vehicle
into something unusual.

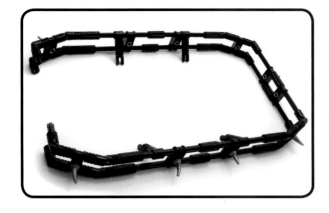

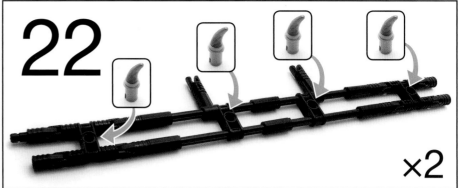

22

×2

23

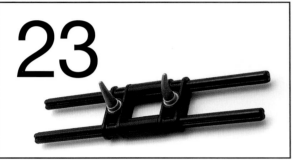

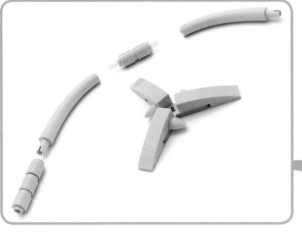

Crumbling Wall

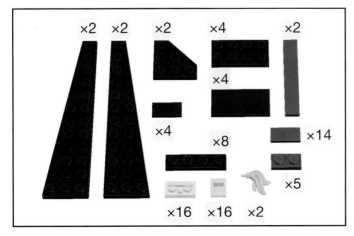

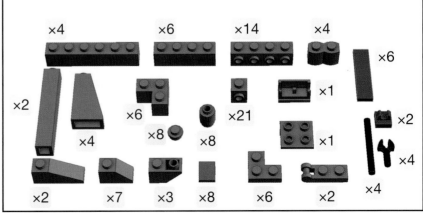

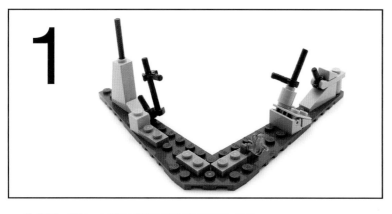

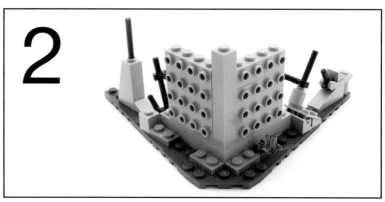

Still Standing

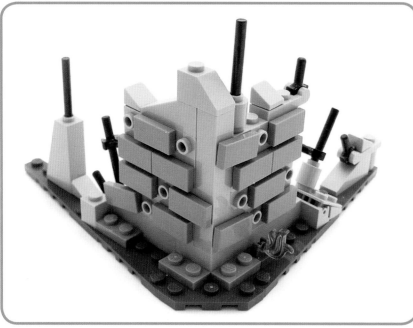

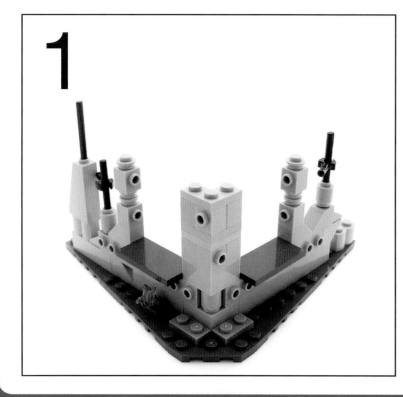

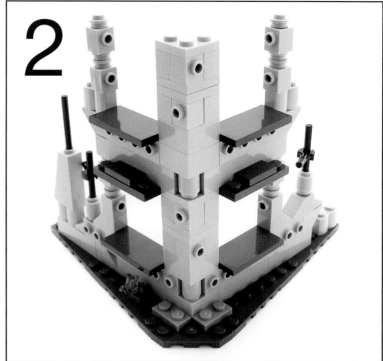

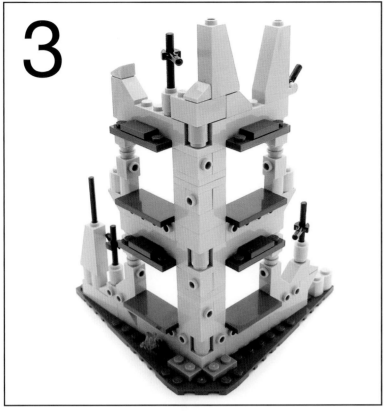

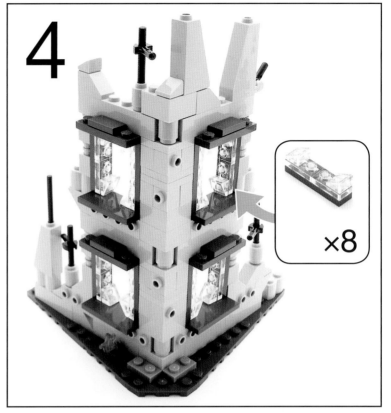

A Veritable Fortress

Marco den Besten

Nickname: 'Ecclesiastes

Profession: Sales Manager

Nationality: Dutch

Website: *www.flickr.com/photos/mcdenbesten/*

Watchtower

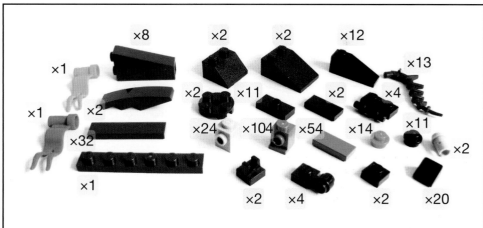

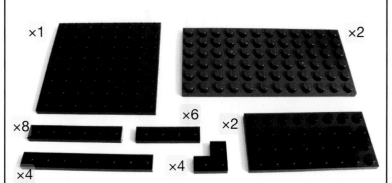

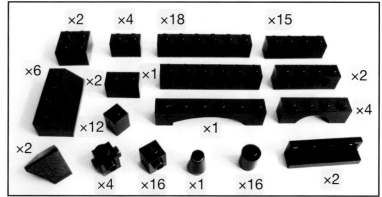

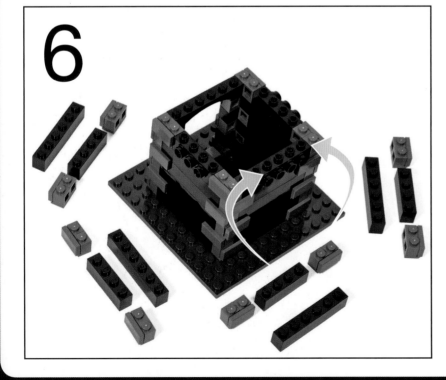

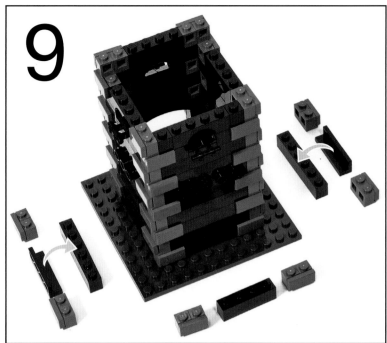

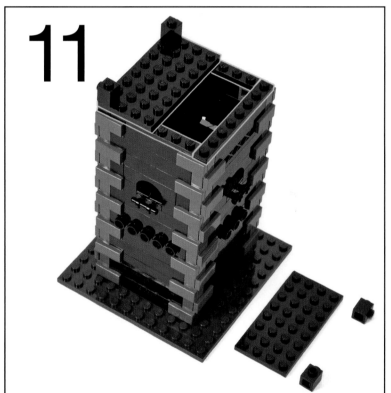

Building Tip
Using an accent color for the cornerstones will give your building more character and create the appearance of ancient stonework.

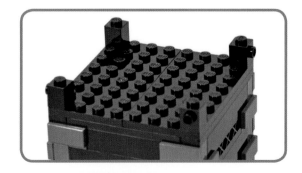

12

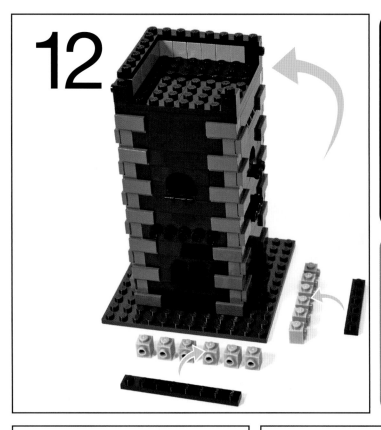

13 ×4

14

15

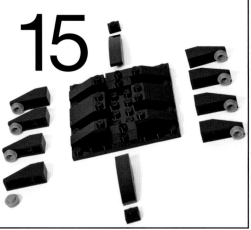

16

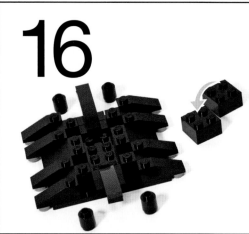

17

18

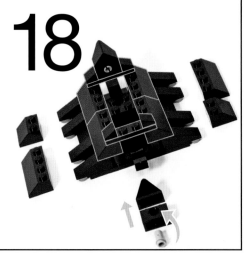

19

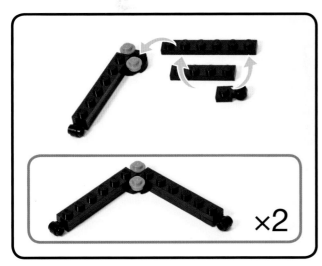

×2

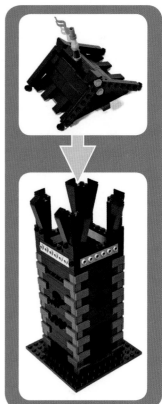

20

×2

Building Tip
Use multiple plant pieces in combination to make trees or add flowers for atmosphere.

NOW THAT WE'VE REBUILT THE TOWER, WE COULD USE SOMETHING TO DEFEND OURSELVES A BIT BETTER.

AH YES. BRILLIANT IDEA, MEGS!

WHY NOT BUILD A CATAPULT? THAT SHOULD SCARE THE DESTRUCTOR AND ANY OTHER MONSTERS ABOUT.

Catapult

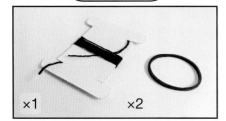

×1   ×2

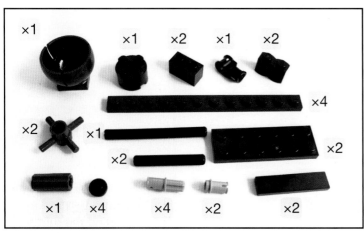

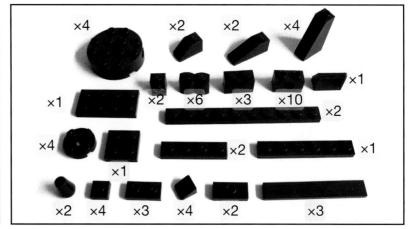

THE CATAPULT IS A BIT COMPLICATED AND REQUIRES SOME STRING AND STRONG RUBBER BANDS. WATCH OUT FOR FLYING DEBRIS WHEN YOU USE IT AND DON'T AIM AT ANYBODY!

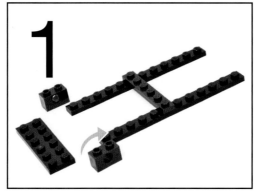

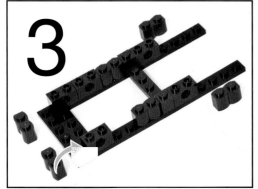

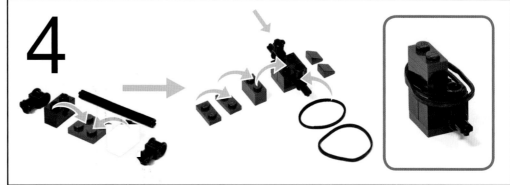

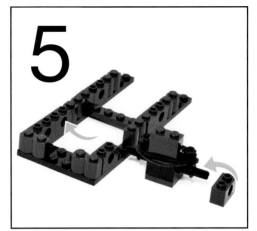

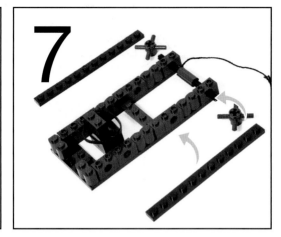

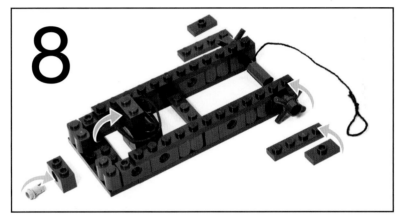

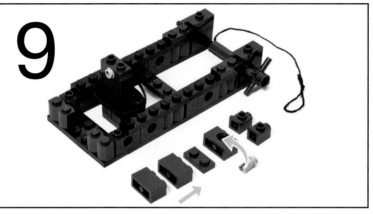

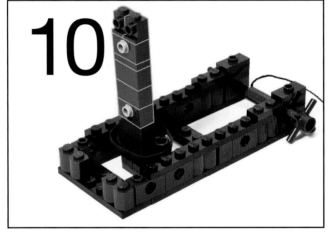

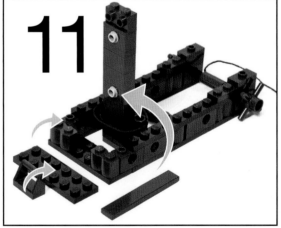

Building Tip
Putting the rubber band on can be a bit tricky. First thread it under the 2×6 plate and pull it over the 1×2 handle, and then adjust it on the catapult.

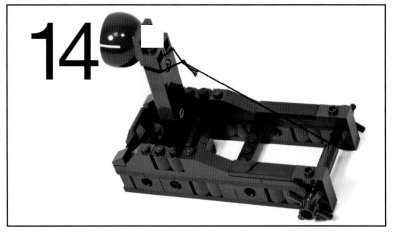

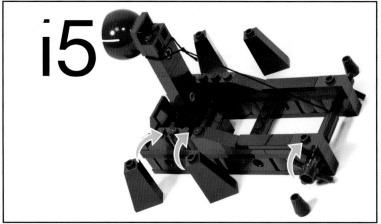

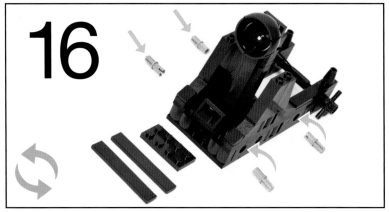

Building Tip
You can add more rubber bands to the catapult to increase its power, but adding too many could break it apart.

BUILDING JOURNAL

Marco has created a very cool world! He often finds inspiration in online building contests. Before he starts building any structures, he uses minifigures to come up with new characters, which are essential to his models. He thinks about what kind of environment they would live in, like snow, mountains, or swamplands, and considers the elevation. After he has built the terrain, he imagines the kind of buildings that would exist there. He plans it all out in his head and then builds each model to suit its environment. When I build, I should consider not only the buildings but their surroundings and how they flow with each other.

ALL THIS BUILDING MAKES ME AND MY MEN VERY HUNGRY. LET'S BUILD A CART TO SEND THE MARKET TO GET SOME FOOD.

Market Cart

GOOD THINKING, MARCO, I HAVEN'T EATEN SINCE I LEFT HOME! I THINK WE'RE ALL HUNGRY NOW.

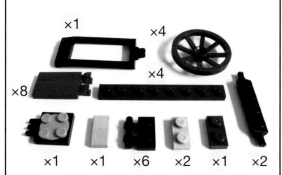

×1 ×4 ×4 ×8

×1 ×1 ×6 ×2 ×1 ×2

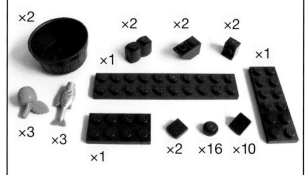

×2 ×2 ×2 ×2 ×1 ×1

×3 ×3 ×1 ×2 ×16 ×10

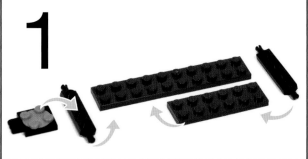

1

2

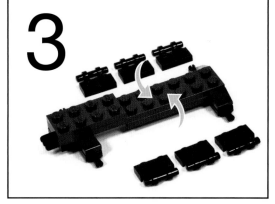

3

4

5

6

×2

7

Building Tip
The sides of the cart can be in any colors. Try giving the cart your own twist.

8

9

10

11

THAT WAS A GOOD FISH DINNER, MARCO, BUT I SHOULD GO AFTER THE DESTRUCTOR NOW.

IT WAS NICE TO MEET YOU, MEGS. THANK YOU FOR YOUR HELP— AND SAFE TRAVELS!

HISTORICA

Guilds of Historica is an online building community. People can join one of the guilds, share their models, and participate in building challenges. Each guild has a different focus, so builders can join one that fits their style and interests. For more information, visit: www.eurobricks.com/forum/index.php?showforum=145/.

Garra Tower

Eaurios

Ondylion City

Brick Friends

Yvonne Doyle

Nickname: {YVD}

Profession: SQL Programmer

Nationality: British

Website: www.flickr.com/photos/yvonnedoyle/

Classic Kitchen

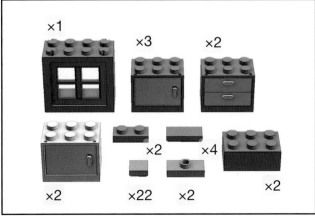

YOU HAVE A LOVELY HOME, YVONNE.

WHY THANK YOU, MEGS, I BUILT THE KITCHEN MYSELF. HERE, I WILL SHOW YOU THE BUILDING PLANS.

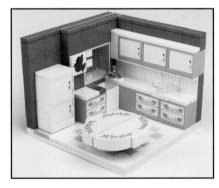

MY KITCHEN CAN BE BUILT IN A LOT OF DIFFERENT COLORS AND WITH DIFFERENT CABINETS. IT'S EASY TO BE AN INTERIOR DESIGNER WITH LEGO BRICKS.

×1 ×3 ×2

×2 ×2 ×4

×2

×2 ×22 ×2 ×2

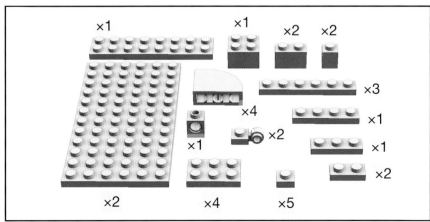

×1 ×1 ×2 ×2

×3

×4 ×1

×1 ×2 ×1

×2

×2 ×4 ×5

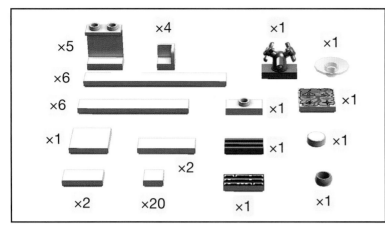

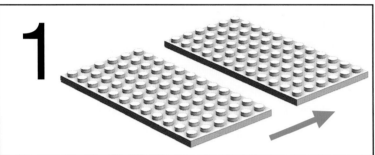

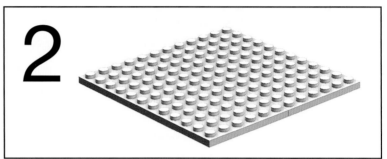

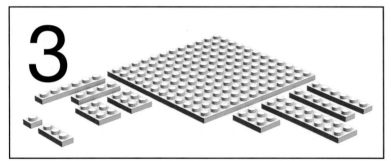

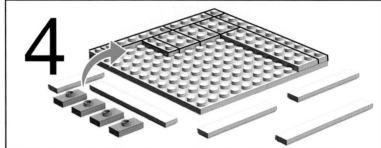

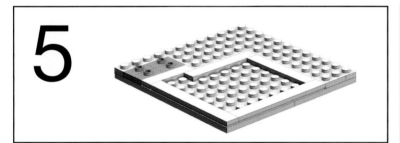

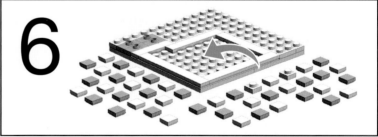

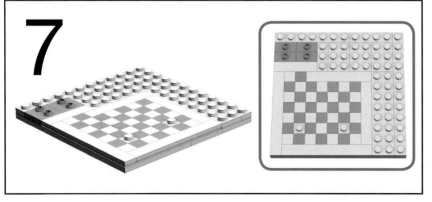

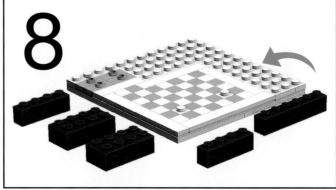

9

10

11 ×2

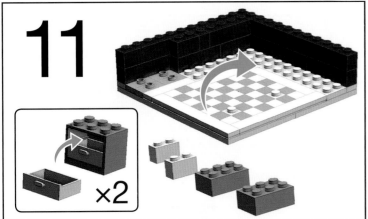

12

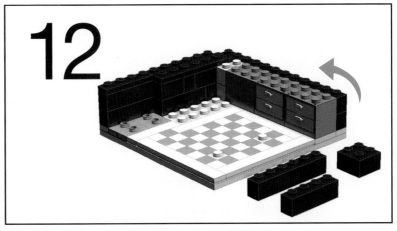

13

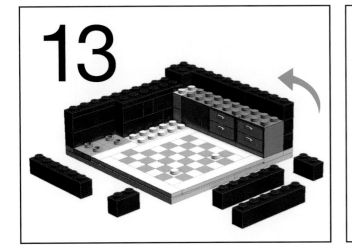

14

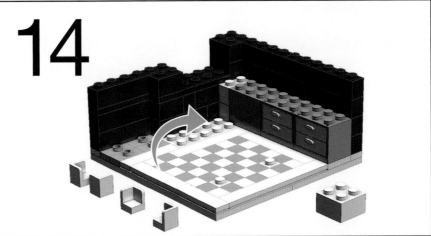

15

16

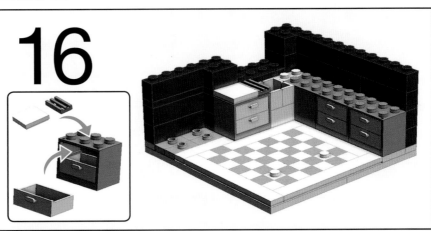

17

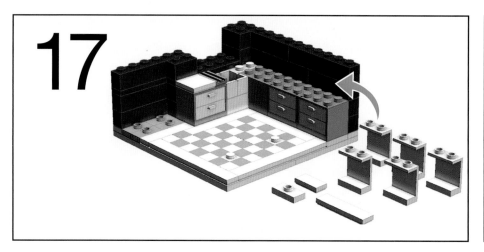

18

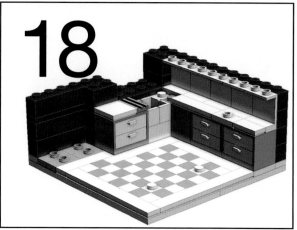

19

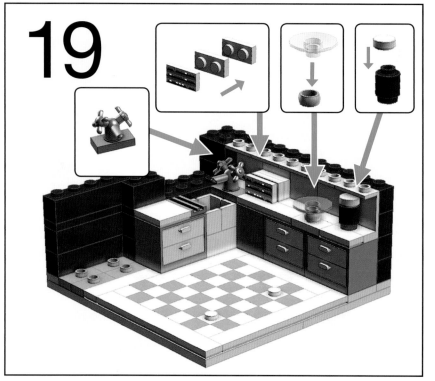

20

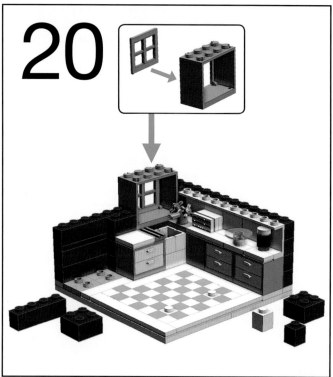

21

22

23

×3

24

25

26

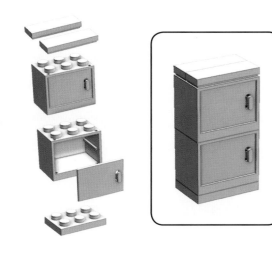

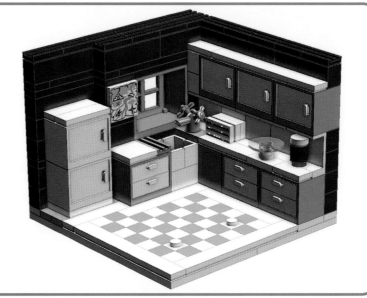

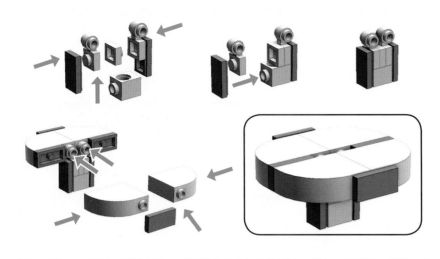

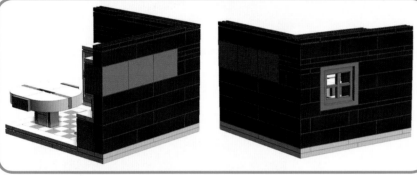

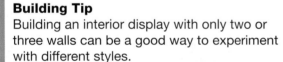

Building Tip
Building an interior display with only two or three walls can be a good way to experiment with different styles.

LOOKS GREAT!

THANK YOU, MEGS, I REALLY ENJOY BUILDING. ANYONE CAN CREATE WITH LEGO BRICKS.

THAT'S RIGHT, YVONNE, ALL IT TAKES IS A BIT OF IMAGINATION!

OH YES, AND A LITTLE BIT OF PRACTICE. AH, THERE, THE CUPCAKES ARE READY. HERE, TRY ONE.

MMM, THESE ARE FANTASTIC! THANKS, YVONNE!

LET'S SEE THE REST OF WOODVALE.

WOW, THESE HOUSES ARE BEAUTIFUL. I'M GLAD I CAME ACROSS YOUR PLACE. I'M ACTUALLY TRACKING A BADDIE WHO CALLS HIMSELF "THE DESTRUCTOR." HE LIKES TO TEAR LEGO MODELS APART.

OH DEAR, I'VE NOT SEEN ANYTHING OUT OF THE ORDINARY HERE.

WELL, WE SHOULD DOUBLE-CHECK TO BE SURE.

LET'S CHECK IN HERE. THIS IS MY LOCAL GYM WHERE I WORK OUT.

YOU CAN BE MY GUEST, AND WE CAN GO FOR A RUN.

CHECK OUT OUR NEW LOCKER ROOMS. I'M SO GLAD THEY WERE REMODELED. THEY USED TO BE THE BOYS' LOCKER ROOMS, AND THEY WERE A BIT SMELLY. HEHE.

THEY LOOK VERY NICE YVONNE. ALL CLEAN AND SHINY NOW!

OUR GYM HAS ALL SORTS OF GREAT EQUIPMENT.

YEAH, THERE IS A LOT OF COOL STUFF HERE.

Treadmill

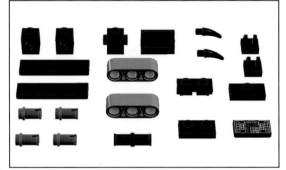

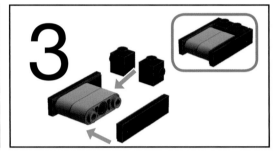

1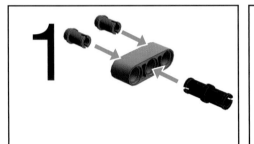

2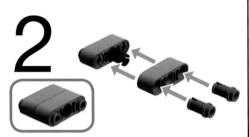

3

4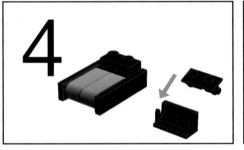

5

6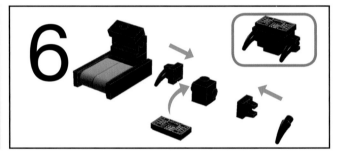

Classroom

Cooking Lessons

A LEGO Legend Calls

Daniel August Krentz

Profession: Retired LEGO Designer

Nationality: American/Danish

Space Bus

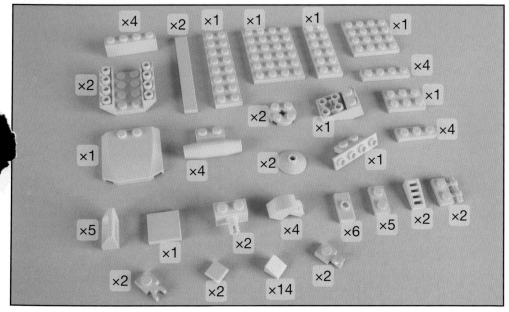

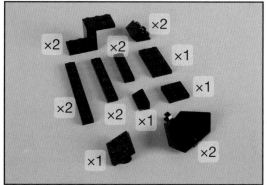

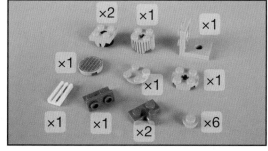

1

2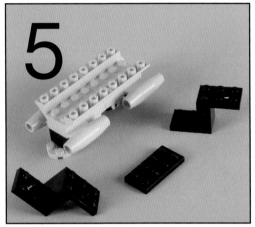

3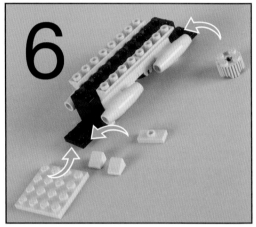

4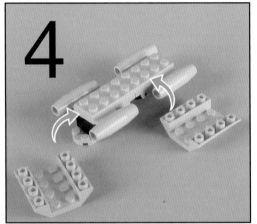

5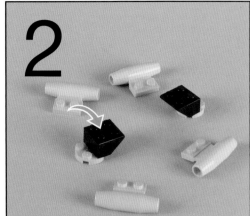

6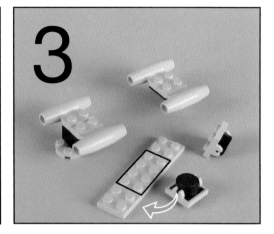

7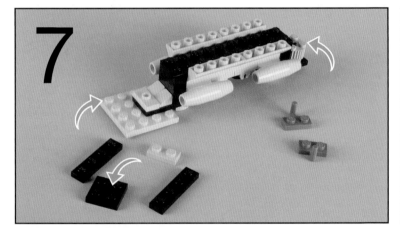

8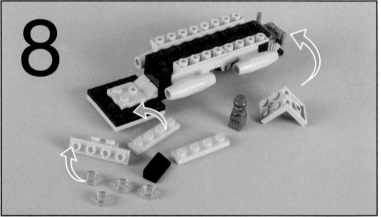

9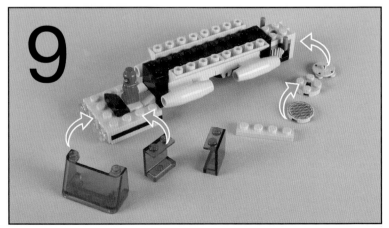

10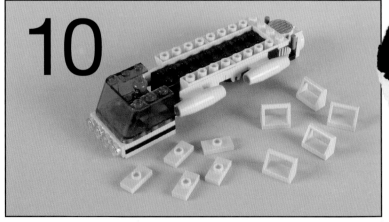

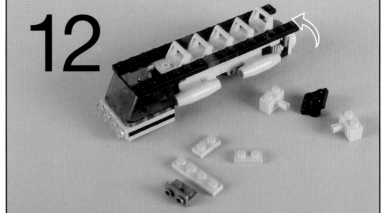

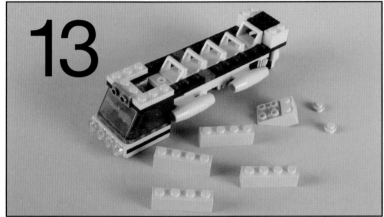

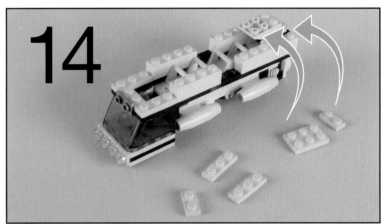

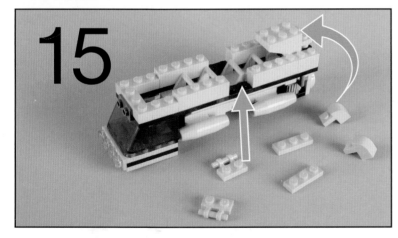

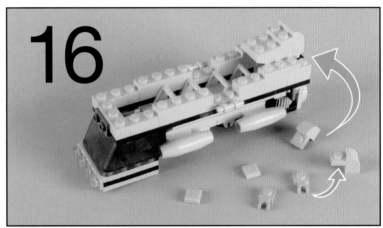

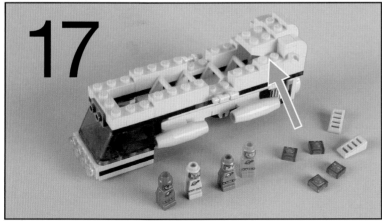

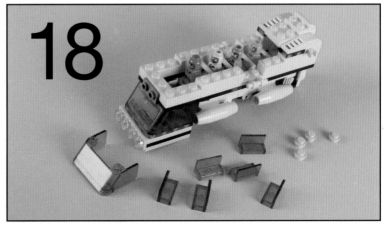

19

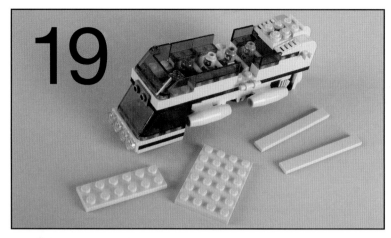

20

21

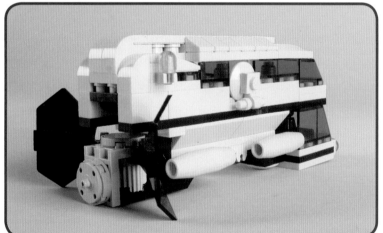

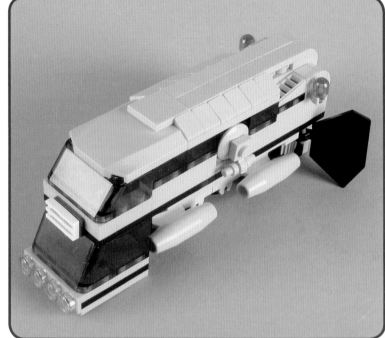

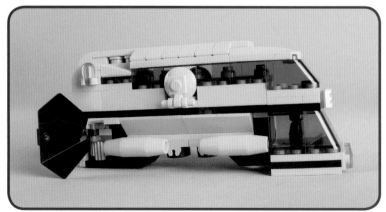

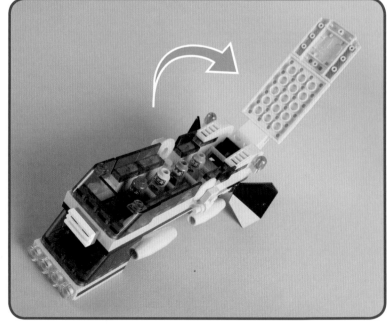